JUNE JORDAN—poet, e̶s̶ born in Harlem and raised in Brooklyn, where she began writing poetry at the age of seven. Her writing has won her much acclaim and many literary awards. In 1969 she received a Rockefeller grant in creative writing; her novel, *His Own Where*, was the finalist for the National Book Award in 1972; and in 1985 she won the New York Foundation for the Arts Fellowship in poetry and a Massachusetts Council for the Arts award for her essay, 'On the Difficult Miracle of Black Poetry in America or Something Like a Sonnet for Phillis Wheatley', included in *Moving Towards Home*, a collection of her political essays, also published by Virago. She travels widely to read her poems and speak on the themes of her writing: politics in the street, Black women, Black literature, child welfare, and education in America. She has taught at CCNY, Sarah Lawrence College and Yale University. She currently teaches at SUNY (Stony Brook) and lives in Brooklyn.

In *Lyrical Campaigns*, a selection of June Jordan's poems we witness the variety and daring of her work—ballads, 'dub' poetry, an unparalleled range of personae and languages, hilarious satire, and witty, precise word choice, rhythm and sound patterning. Her poems address and attack predatory politics and still others offer up elegies for Chile, Guatemala, Palestine. She sings of heroes, heroines, and victims. She sings of sexual desire and power. June Jordan is a lyrical catalyst for change.

LYRICAL CAMPAIGNS
Selected Poems

JUNE JORDAN

My loving thanks to Mark Ainley and to Pratibha Parmar:
two new, best friends who help me keep the faith.

Published by VIRAGO PRESS Limited 1989
20–23 Mandela Street, Camden Town, London NW1 0HQ

Reprinted 1989

Copyright © June Jordan 1980, 1981, 1985

All rights reserved

These poems have been previously published in *Passion*
(Beacon Press, 1980), *Things that I do in the Dark*
(Beacon Press, 1981) and *Living Room*
(Thunder's Mouth Press, 1985)

A CIP catalogue record of this book
is available from the British Library

Photoset by Rowland Phototypesetting Limited
Bury St Edmunds, Suffolk
Printed in Great Britain by
The Guernsey Press Co. Ltd,
Guernsey, Channel Islands

For Adrienne

Contents

PART ONE: from *Things That I Do in the Dark*

Who Look at Me   *3*

For My Jamaican Sister a Little Bit Lost on the Island of Manhattan   *12*

Juice of a Lemon on the Trail of Little Yellow   *12*

One Minus One Minus One   *13*

On the Spirit of Mildred Jordan   *13*

Ah, Momma   *14*

From *The Talking Back of Miss Valentine Jones:* Poem # one   *15*

The Wedding   *18*

The Reception   *18*

Roman Poem Number Eight   *19*

Roman Poem Number Thirteen   *20*

Roman Poem Number Fourteen   *21*

For My Brother   *22*

It's About You: On the Beach   *22*

Of Nightsong and Flight   *23*

About Long Distances on Saturday   *24*

Calling on All Silent Minorities   *24*

No Poem Because Time Is Not a Name   *25*

On a New Year's Eve   *26*

For Ethelbert   *29*

For Dave: 1976 *30*
Meta-Rhetoric *31*
On the Loss of Energy (and other things) *32*
What Would I Do White? *35*
In Memoriam: Martin Luther King, Jr. *36*
For Michael Angelo Thompson (October 25, 1959–March 23, 1973) *37*
On Moral Leadership as a Political Dilemma (Watergate, 1973) *39*
Uhuru in the O.R. *41*
If You Saw a Negro Lady *41*
Roman Poem Number Five *42*
Roman Poem Number Six *54*
About Enrique's Drawing *56*
On Declining Values *57*
Some People *59*
Fragments from a Parable *59*

PART TWO: from *Passion*
For the Sake of a People's Poetry: Walt Whitman and the Rest of Us *69*
Current Events *79*
Case in Point *80*
Newport Jazz Festival *81*
Patricia's Poem *82*
Letter to the Local Police *83*
Poem about Police Violence *84*
Sketching in the Transcendental *85*

A Poem about Intelligence for My Brothers and Sisters *86*
1977: Poem for Mrs. Fannie Lou Hamer *87*
Poem for South African Women *89*
Unemployment Monologue *90*
A Song of Sojourner Truth *91*
Alla Tha's All Right, but *93*
Free Flight *93*
Letter to My Friend the Poet Ntozake Shange *97*
En Passant *97*
A Short Note to My Very Critical and Well-Beloved Friends and Comrades *98*
Rape is Not a Poem *98*
Memo: *100*
What is This in Reference To? or We Must Get Together Sometime Soon! *101*
Poem about My Rights *102*
Grand Army Plaza *104*

PART THREE: from *Living Room*

From Sea to Shining Sea *109*
Des Moines Iowa Rap *114*
First Poem from Nicaragua Libre: *teotecacinte* *115*
From Nicaragua Libre: photograph of managua *116*
Problems of Translation: Problems of Language *117*
Poem on the Road; for Alice Walker *120*
A Song for Soweto *122*
Song of the Law Abiding Citizen *124*
October 23, 1983 *125*

Menu *126*
Addenda to the Papal Bull *128*
Poem for Guatemala *129*
On the Real World: Meditation # 1 *131*
Poem on *132*
A Runaway Lil Bit Poem *132*
DeLiza Questioning Perplexities *133*
Poem Towards a Final Solution *133*
Apologies to All the People in Lebanon *135*
Another Poem About the Man *137*
Poor Form *138*
The Test of Atlanta 1979— *138*
Relativity *140*
Home: January 29, 1984 *140*
Nightline: September 20, 1982 *141*
Moving Towards Home *142*

PART ONE

FROM
*Things that I Do
in the Dark*

Who Look at Me
Dedicated to my son, Christopher

Who would paint a people
black or white?

*

For my own I have held
where nothing showed me how
where finally I left alone
to trace another destination

*

A white stare splits the air
by blindness on the subway
in department stores
The Elevator
           (that unswerving ride
where man ignores the brother
by his side)

A white stare splits obliterates
the nerve-wrung wrist from work
the breaking ankle or
the turning glory
of a spine

*

Is that how we look to you
a partial nothing clearly real?

Who see a solid clarity
of feature
size and shape of some
one head
an unmistaken nose

the fact of afternoon
as darkening
his candle eyes

Older men with swollen neck
(when they finally sit down
who will stand up
for them?)

I cannot remember nor imagine pretty
people treat me
like a doublejointed stick
                    WHO LOOK AT ME
                    WHO SEE
the tempering sweetness
of a little girl who wears
her first pair of earrings
and a red dress

the grace of a boy removing
a white mask he makes beautiful

Iron grille across the glass
and frames of motion closed or
charred or closed

The axe lies on the ground
She listening to his coming sound

Him
just touching his feet
powerful and wary

anonymous and normal
parents and their offspring
posed in formal
                    *
I am
impossible to explain
remote from old and new interpretations
and yet
not exactly
                    *
look at the stranger as

he lies more gray than black
on that colorquilt
that
(everyone will say)
seems bright beside him

look
black sailors on the light
green sea the sky keeps blue

the wind blows high
and hard at night
for anyhow anywhere new
*
Who see starvation at the table
lines of men no work to do
my mother ironing a shirt?

Who see a frozen skin the midnight
of the winter and the hallway cold
to kill you like the dirt?

where kids buy soda pop
in shoeshine parlors
barber shops so they can hear
some laughing

Who look at me?

Who see the children
on their street the torn down door the wall
complete an early losing
                        games of ball
the search to find
a fatherhood a mothering of mind
a multimillion multicolored mirror
of an honest humankind?
*
look close
and see me black man mouth
for breathing (North and South)
A MAN

I am black alive and looking back at you.
*
see me brown girl throat
that throbs from servitude

see me hearing fragile
leap
and lead a black boy
reckless to succeed
to wrap my pride
around tomorrow and to go

there
without fearing

see me darkly covered ribs
around my heart across my skull
thin skin protects the part
that dulls from longing

*

Who see the block we face
the thousand miles of solid alabaster space
inscribed keep off keep out don't touch
and Wait Some More for Half as Much?

*

To begin is no more agony
than opening your hand

*

sometimes you have to dance
like spelling
the word joyless

*

Describe me broken mast
adrift but strong
regardless what may
come along

*

What do you suppose he hears
every evening?

*

I am stranded in a hungerland
of great prosperity

*

shelter happens seldomly and
like an accident
it stops

*

No doubt
the jail is white where I was born
but black will bail me out

*

We have lived as careful
as a church and prayer
in public

*

we reveal
a complicated past
of tinderbox and ruin
where we carried water
for the crops

we come from otherwhere

victim to a rabid cruel cargo crime

to separate and rip apart
the trusting members of one heart

my family

I looked for you
I looked for you

*

(slavery:) the insolence

*

came to frontiers
of paralyze highways
freedom strictly underground

came here to hatred hope labor love
and lynchlength rope

came a family to a family

*

I found my father
silently despite the grieving
fury of his life

Afternoons he wore his hat
and held a walking stick

I found my mother
her geography
becomes our home

*

so little safety
almost nowhere like the place
that childhood plans
in a pounding happy space
between deliberate brown and clapping
hands

that preached a reaping to the wildly
    sleeping earth
brown hands that worked for rain a fire inside
    and food to eat
from birth brown hands
    to hold

       *

New energies of darkness we
disturbed a continent
like seeds

and life grows slowly
so we grew

We became a burly womb
an evening harvest kept by prayers
a hallelujah little room

We grew despite the crazy killing scorn
that broke the brightness to be born

In part we grew
by looking back at you

that white terrain
impossible for black America to thrive
that hostile soil to mazelike toil
backbreaking people into pain

we grew by work by waiting
to be seen
black face black body and black mind
beyond obliterating
homicide of daily insult daily death
the pistol slur the throbbing redneck war
with breath

In part we grew
with heroes who could halt a slaveship
lead the crew
like Cinque (son
of a Mendi African Chief) he
led in 1839
the Amistad Revolt

from slavehood forced
a victory he
killed the captain killed the cook
took charge
a mutiny for manhood
people
called him killer but
some
the Abolitionists
looked back at robbery
of person
murdering of spirit
slavery requires
and one
John Quincy Adams (seventy-three)
defended Cinque who
by highest court decree
in 1841 stood free
and freely he returned
to Africa
victorious

In part we grew
grandmother husband son
together when the laborblinding day was done

In part we grew
as we were meant to grow
ourselves
with kings and queens no white man knew

we grew by sitting on a stolen chair
by windows and a dream
by setting up a separate sail
to carry life
to start the song

to stop the scream

*

These times begin the ending of all lies
the fantasies of seasons start and stop
the circle leads to no surprise
for death does not bewilder

only life can kill can mystify can start
and stop like flowers ripening a funeral
like (people) holding hands across the knife
that cuts the casket to an extraordinary size

*

Tell the whiplash helmets GO!
and take away
that cream and orange Chevrolet
stripped to inside steel and parked
forever on one wheel

Set the wild dogs chewing up
that pitiful capitulation
plastic flower plastic draperies
to dust the dirt

Break the clothesline
Topple down the clotheslinepole

O My Lives Among The Wounded Buildings
should be dressed in trees and grass

*

we will no longer wait for want for watch
for what we will

*

we make a music marries room to room.

*

listen to that new girl
tears her party dress to sweep
the sidewalk as the elderly slow
preacher nears the mailbox in a black suit
emptyhanded

*

Although the world
forgets me
I will say yes
AND NO

*

NO
to a carnival run by freaks
who take a life
and tie it terrible
behind my back

No One Exists As Number Two
If you deny it you should try
being someone number two

*

I want to hear something other than a single
ringing on the concrete

*

I grieve the sorrow roar the sorrow sob
of many more left hand or right
black children and white
men the mountaintop the mob
I grieve the sorrow roar the sorrow sob
the fractured staring at the night

Sometimes America the shamescape
knock-rock territory losing shape
the Southern earth like blood
rolls valleys cold gigantic
weeping willow flood
that lunatic that lovely land
that graveyard growing
trees remark where men
another black man
died he died again
he died

*

I trust you will remember how we tried to love
above the pocket deadly need to please
and how so many of us died there
on our knees

*

Who see the roof and corners of my pride
to be (as you are) free?

WHO LOOK AT ME?

For My Jamaican Sister a Little Bit Lost on the Island of Manhattan

small
and glowing in this cold place
of brick
   cement
   dry sand
   and
   broken glass
where there are waters
of the earth
flowing like love alive
you will make them warm
waters
hot (even)
like the delicate sweat
of tiger lilies
blowing about
barely in flame
               at sunrise

Juice of a Lemon on the Trail of Little Yellow

Little Yellow looked at the banana tree and
he looked at the moon and he heard a banana tree baboon
beneath the moon and he sat on the grass
and fell asleep there

Little Yellow nine years old underneath the moon beside
a big banana tree smiled a mango smile as he
listened to a lullabye palm and a naked woman broke
coconuts for him and fed him meat from her mango
mammaries
Little Yellow curled himself in a large banana leaf
and he deeply sailed asleep toward the mango moon

Little Yellow traveled to a place where coolies worked
to build a bathtub for the rough and tribal Caribbean

There on that lush cerulean plateau and trapped he
was kept by his boss brother who positively took
out his teeth and left the mango mouth of Little Yellow
empty

One Minus One Minus One
(This is a first map of territory I will have to explore as poems, again and again)

My mother murdering me
to have a life of her own

What would I say
(if I could speak about it?)

My father raising me
to be a life that he
owns

What can I say
(in this loneliness)

On The Spirit of Mildred Jordan

After sickness and a begging
from her bed
my mother dressed herself
grey lace-up oxfords
stockings baggy on her shrunken legs
an orange topper
rhinestone buttons
and a powder blue straw
hat with plastic
flowers

Then
she took the street
in short steps toward the corner

chewing gum
no less

she let the family laugh
again

she wasn't foxy
she was strong

Ah, Momma

Ah, Momma,
Did the house ever know the night-time of your spirit: the flash and flame of you who once, when we crouched in what you called "the little room," where your dresses hung in their pallid colorings—an uninteresting row of uniforms—and where there were dusty, sweet-smelling boxes of costume jewelry that nevertheless shone like rubies, gold, and diamonds, once, in that place where the secondhand mirror blurred the person, dull, that place without windows, with doors instead of walls, so that your small-space most resembled a large and rather hazardous closet, once, in there you told me, whispering, that once, you had wanted to be an artist: someone, you explained, who could just boldly go and sit near the top of a hill and watch the setting of the sun
Ah, Momma!
You said this had been your wish when you were quite as young as I was then: a twelve- or thirteen-year-old girl who heard your confidence with terrified amazement: what had happened to you and your wish? Would it happen to me too?

Ah, Momma:
  "The little room" of your secrets, your costumery, perfumes and photographs of an old boyfriend you did not marry (for reasons not truly clear to me as I saw you make sure, time after time, that his pictures were being kept as clean and as safely as possible)—"the little

room" adjoined the kitchen, the kitchen where no mystery survived, except for the mystery of you: woman who covered her thick and long, black hair with a starched, white nurse's cap when she went "on duty" away from our home into the hospital I came to hate, jealously, woman who rolled up her wild and heavy, beautiful hair before she went to bed, woman who tied a headrag around the waving, kinky, well-washed braids, or lengthy, fat curls of her hair while she moved, without particular grace or light, between the table and the stove, between the sink and the table, around and around and around in the spacious, ugly kitchen where she, where you, never dreamed about what you were doing or what you might do instead, and where you taught me to set down plates and silverware, and even fresh-cut flowers from the garden, without appetite, without excitement, without expectation.

   It was not there, in that obvious, open, square cookery where you spent most of the hours of the days, it was not there, in the kitchen where nothing ever tasted sweet or sharp enough to sate the yearnings I began to suspect inside your eyes, and also inside the eyes of my father, it was not there that I began to hunger for the sun as my own, legitimate preoccupation; it was not there, in the kitchen, that I began, really, to love you
Ah, Momma,
It was where I found you, hidden away, in your "little room," where your life and the power, the rhythms of your sacrifice, the ritual of your bowed head, and your laughter always partly concealed, where all of you, womanly, reverberated big as the whole house, it was there that I came, humbly, into an angry, an absolute determination that I would, one day, prove myself to be, in fact, your daughter
Ah, Momma, I am still trying

From The Talking Back of Miss Valentine Jones: *Poem # one*

well I wanted to braid my hair
bathe and bedeck my
self so fine
so fully aforethought for
your pleasure
see:
I wanted to travel and read

and runaround fantastic
into war and peace:
I wanted to
surf
dive
fly
climb
conquer
and be conquered
THEN
I wanted to pickup the phone
and find you asking me
if I might possibly be alone
some night
(so I could answer cool
as the jewels I would wear
on bareskin for your
digmedaddy delectation:)
"WHEN
you comin ova?"
But
I had to remember to write down
margarine on the list
and shoepolish and a can of
sliced pineapples in casea company
and a quarta skim milk cause Teresa's
gaining weight and don' nobody groove on
that much
girl
and next I hadta sort for darks and lights before
the laundry hit the water which I had
to kinda keep a eye on be-
cause if the big hose jumps the sink again that
Mrs. Thompson gointa come upstairs
and brain me with a mop don' smell too
nice even though she hang
it headfirst out the winda
and I had to check
on William like to
burn hisself to death with fever
boy so thin be
callin all day "Momma! Sing to me?"

"Ma! Am I gone die?" and me not
wake enough to sit beside him longer than
to wipeaway the sweat or change the sheets/
his shirt and feed him orange
juice before I fall out sleep and
Sweet My Jesus ain but one can
left
and we not thru the afternoon
and now
you (temporarily) shownup with a thing
you say's a poem and you
call it
"Will The Real Miss Black America Standup?"

                      guilty po' mouth
                      about duty beauties of my
                      headrag
                      boozedup doozies about
                      never mind
                      cause love is blind

well
I can't use it

and the very next bodacious Blackman
call me queen
because my life ain shit
because (in any case) he ain been here to share it
with me
(dish for dish and do for do and
dream for dream)
I'm gone scream him out my house
be-
cause what I wanted was
to braid my hair/bathe and bedeck my
self so fully be-
cause what I wanted was
your love
not pity
be-
cause what I wanted was
your love
your love

The Wedding

Tyrone married her this afternoon
not smiling as he took the aisle
and her slightly rough hand.
Dizzella listened to the minister
staring at his wrist and twice
forgetting her name:
Do you promise to obey?
Will you honor humility and love
as poor as you are?
Tyrone stood small but next
to her person
trembling. Tyrone stood
straight and bony
black alone with one key
in his pocket.
By marrying today
they made themselves a man
and woman
answered friends or unknown
curious about the Cadillacs
displayed in front of Beaulah Baptist.
Beaulah Baptist
life in general
indifferent
barely known
nor caring to consider
the earlywed Tyrone
and his Dizzella
brave enough
but only two.

The Reception

Doretha wore the short blue lace last night
and William watched her drinking so she fight
with him in flying collar slim-jim orange
tie and alligator belt below the navel pants uptight

"I flirt. You hear me? Yes I flirt.
Been on my pretty knees all wcck
to clean the rich white downtown dirt
the greedy garbage money reek.

I flirt. Damned right. You look at me."
But William watched her carefully
his mustache shaky she could see
him jealous, "which is how he always be

at parties." Clementine and Wilhelmina
looked at trouble in the light blue lace
and held to Geroge while Roosevelt Senior
circled by the yella high and bitterly light blue face

he liked because she worked
the crowded room like clay like molding men
from dust to muscle jerked
and arms and shoulders moving when

she moved. The Lord Almighty Seagrams bless
Doretha in her short blue dress
and Roosevelt waiting for his chance:
a true gut-funky blues to make her really dance.

Roman Poem Number Eight

He ordered a beer
She ordered a beer
I asked for apricot
yoghurt
      "You know this game?
Nothing personal. For instance
June is all bird
but you," he spoke
to my rival, "You
are half-horse-half-
butterfly."
        "Why
do you say I'm a bird?"

"Always up in the head
thinking
far from the earth."

I had been counting
the hairs on his wrist
but today
since he has been really
riding his horse
I venture to startle
the hairs of his arm
and listen to the thick
crackling
of his
persistent sex.

Roman Poem Number Thirteen
For Eddie

Only our hearts will argue hard
against the small lights letting in the news
and who can choose between the worst possibility
and the last
between the winners of the wars against the breathing
and the last
war everyone will lose
and who can choose between the dry gas
domination of the future
and the past
between the consequences of the killers
and the past
of all the killing? There
is no choice in these.
Your voice
breaks very close to me my love.

Roman Poem Number Fourteen

believe it love
believe
      my lover
lying down he
lifts me up and high
and I am
high on him

believe it love
believe

the carnage scores around
the corner

o believe it love
believe

the bleeding fills the carnage cup
my lover lifts me
I am up
      and love is lying down

believe
believe it

crazies wear a clean shirt to the fire
o my lover
lift me higher higher

crazies take a scream and
make a speech they talk and
wash their mouths in dirt
no love will hurt
me lover lift me lying down

believe
believe it
carnage crazies
snap smash more more
(what you waiting for?)

you own the rope knife rifles the whole list
the searing bomb starch brighteners
the nuclear family whiteners

look the bridge be fallen down
look the ashes from the bones turn brown
look the mushroom hides the town
look the general wears his drip dry red
drip gown

o my lover nakedly
believe my love

believe
believe it

For My Brother

Teach me to sing
Blackman Blacklove
sing when the cops break your head
full of song
sing when the bullets explode in the back
you bend over me
Blacklove Blackman
sing when you empty the world
to fill up the needles that kill
needles killing you
killing
you
teach me to sing
Blackman Blacklove
teach me to sing.

It's About You:
On the Beach

You have
two hands absolutely lean and clean
to let go the gold
the silver flat or plain rock

sand
but hold the purple pieces
atom articles
that glorify a color
yours is orange
oranges are like you love
a promising
a calm skin and a juice
inside
a juice
a running from the desert
Lord
see how you run
YOUR BODY IS A LONG BLACK WING
YOUR BODY IS A LONG BLACK WING

Of Nightsong and Flight

There are things lovely and dangerous still

the rain
when the heat of an evening
sweetens the darkness with mist

and the eyes cannot see what the memory will
of new pain

when the headlights deceive
like the windows wild birds believe to be air
and bash bodies and wings
on the glass

when the headlights show space
but the house and the room and the bed and your face
are still there
while I am mistaken
and try to drive by

the actual kiss
of the world everywhere

About Long Distances on Saturday

he calls me from his house and
the timing seems bad
and I offer to call him back
later
but he says "no"
I'm about to split for the weekend
so
call me yeah
early next week or
sometime
and the answer is
that the question
is

(isn't it)

where are you going
baby

without me?

Calling on All Silent Minorities

HEY

C'MON
COME OUT

WHEREVER YOU ARE

WE NEED TO HAVE THIS MEETING
AT THIS TREE

AIN' EVEN BEEN
PLANTED
YET

No Poem Because Time Is Not a Name

But beyond the
anxiety
the
querulous and reckless intersecting
conflict
and the trivial misleading banal
and separating fences every scrim
disguise each mask and feint
red herrings broadside poor
maneuvers of the
begging
hopeful
heart that wants and waits the
head that works against the minute
minute
There are pictures/memories of
temperature or cast or tone
or hue and vision
pictures of a dream
and dreams of memories and
dreams of gardens dreams of film
and pictures
of the daring
simple
fabulous
bold
difficult
and distant
inextricable
main
nigger
that I love
and
this is not
a poem

On a New Year's Eve

Infinity doesn't interest me

not altogether
anymore

I crawl and kneel and grub about
I beg and listen for

what can go away

                (as easily as love)

or perish
like the children
running
hard on oneway streets/infinity
doesn't interest me

not anymore

not even
repetition your/my/eye-
lid or the colorings of sunrise
or all the sky excitement
added up

is not enough

to satisfy this lusting adulation that I feel
for
your brown arm before it
moves

MOVES
CHANGES UP

the temporary sacred
tales ago
first bikeride round the house
when you first saw a squat
opossum
carry babies on her back

opossum up
in the persimmon tree
you reeling toward
that natural
first
absurdity
with so much wonder still
it shakes your voice

                      the temporary is the sacred
                      takes me out

and even the stars and even the snow and even
the rain
do not amount to much
unless these things submit to some disturbance
some derangement such
as when I yield myself/belonging
to your unmistaken
body

and let the powerful lock up the canyon/mountain
peaks the
hidden rivers/waterfalls the
deepdown minerals/the coalfields/goldfields/
diamond mines close by the whoring ore
hot
at the center of the earth

spinning fast as numbers
I cannot imagine

let the world blot
obliterate remove so-
called
magnificence
so-called
almighty/fathomless and everlasting
treasures/
wealth
(whatever that may be)
it is this time
that matters

it is this history
I care about

the one we make together
awkward
inconsistent
as a lame cat on the loose
or quick as kids freed by the bell
or else as strictly
once
as only life must mean
a once upon a time

I have rejected propaganda teaching me
about the beautiful
the truly rare

(supposedly
the soft push of the ocean at the hushpoint of the shore
supposedly
the soft push of the ocean at the hushpoint of the shore
is beautiful
for instance)
but
the truly rare can stay out there

I have rejected that
abstraction that enormity
unless I see a dog walk on the beach/
a bird seize sandflies
or yourself
approach me
laughing out a sound to spoil
the pretty picture
make an uncontrolled
heartbeating memory
instead

I read the papers preaching on
that oil and oxygen
that redwoods and the evergreens
that trees the waters and the atmosphere
compile a final listing of the world in
short supply

but all live and all the lives
persist perpetual
in jeopardy
persist
as scarce as every one of us
as difficult to find
or keep
as irreplaceable
as frail
as every one of us

and
as I watch your arm/your
brown arm
just
before it moves

I know

all things are dear
that disappear

*all things are dear
that disappear*

For Ethelbert

if I cda known youd be real
back in them supreme court
gonna rule all evil out
days
I wda rushd to judgment
(lordy lord)
rushd thru
to the fiery seat itselve
and stayd there
cool as any momma madeup
her holy/everlastin min'
(chile *honey!*)
and sed

"sentence me, please,
to a long life long
enough
so's I gets to meet
what's comin afta (this mess)"
meanin'
you

For Dave: 1976

There wasn't any hot water for the teapot
so you came by to fix the furnace
and you found me
"very pretty" (you said)
underneath my worries

Leaving the wind behind the door you came
and when you left to sleep elsewhere
you left me ready to keep on
dancing by myself

I was accustomed to the Army cap that spills your
hair below those clean-as-a-whistle ears nobody
knows how to blow so you can hear them honest-to-
God
But I was a stranger to your hair let free your arms
around me
reading my lips then licking them gentle as a bear
sure that he hugs a honey tree not going anywhere
(which is true: for you
                    washing up with Ajax
leaving the rifle outside the way the Japanese
leave shoes
catching eels to smoke them good enough to eat
rebuilding a friend's house "after work")

Now you were lifting me as easily as we could laugh
between ourselves
you wanting to know what I was thinking about

me wanting to tell but unwilling to shout
at you (so you could hear me)

You arrive (red shirt
        new shoes
            the shower shining everywhere about you)
And I accept again
that there are simple ways of being joined
to someone
absolutely different from myself
And I admire the forthright
crocus first to mitigate the winter
with its thrust voluptuous/
on time

I mean to say
that it's not talk that brings us close together
and
thank god!

Meta-Rhetoric

Homophobia
racism
self-definition
revolutionary struggle

the subject tonight for
public discussion is
our love

we sit apart
apparently at opposite ends of a line
and I feel the distance
between my eyes
between my legs
a dry
dust topography of our separation

In the meantime people
dispute the probabilities
of union

They reminisce about the chasmic histories
no ideology yet dares to surmount

I disagree with you
You disagree with me
The problem seems to be a matter of scale

Can you give me the statistical dimensions
of your mouth on my mouth
your breasts resting on my own?

I believe the agenda involves
several inches (at least)
of coincidence and endless recovery

My hope is that our lives will declare
this meeting
open

On the Loss of Energy
(and other things)

no more the chicken and the egg come

one of them
before the other
both
be fadin (steady)
from the supersafeway/a & p/giant
circus

>   uh-huh
>   the pilgrim cornucopia
>   it ain' a pot to pee in
>   much
>   (these days)

gas is gone
and alka seltza runnin gas
a close race

outasight/you
name it
      toilet paper
      halfway honest politicians
there's shortage
folks/*please*
step right up)
a crisis
(*come in closer*)
A International Disaster
Definitely Takin Place
(give the little lady down in front some room)
and (*how about the brother in the back row/can*
you hear me brother?)
                WELL
                I SAID THE HOT AIR'S RUNNIN
                OUTASTEAM
                I SAID
                THE MEAT'S NOT GOOD
                FOR KIDS TO EAT
                TOO FULLAFAT
                AND STUFF LIKE THAT
                AND
                IF YOU EAT MEAT
                HOW YOU PLAN TO PAY THE
                   RENT?
                I SAID
                THE OILWELLS DRIBBLIN
                LOWER THAN A SNAKE
                AND SOON WON'T BE NO HEAT
                AND SO YOU MIGHT AS WELL
                   EAT MEAT
                EXCEPT THERE AINT NO
                MEAT TO EAT
                I SAID

                BROTHER CAN YOU SPARE A
                   DIME?

these things/they gettin more and more worse in
the time it takes to tell
you

how the country's bound to hell
you
first
if you be middlin poor or poor or Black or Black-and-poor
this profit-makin mess the worst
mess we been force to handle
since the civil war
close down the crackers
reconstructed
how the north won
into victory the crackers like to celebrate/a
reconstruction of the facts
on poor and Blackbacks
but
I am digressin/*folks*
please settle down and listen good
I say you know
you know
the affluent society
starvin high
on the hog as pigs can get
I say you know
we all been pigs
but mostly we been little pigs/I say
the big pigs
got the whole big pigpen
underneath some tasty big-pig pigs' feet
dynamite can move
where is the dynamite?
How come we tryin to cooperate
with this "emergency"/this faker/phony
ripoff
got you plannin
not to die and not to have a baby
on the weekends
not to do too much/
much less to start to die or start to have
a baby
on a Sunday
or on early Monday
got you/stiff and slow and hungry
on them lines the richboys laugh about/

Will somebody
real and prominent and smart
please stand
up here
and tell about inequities and big and little pigs
and other animals and birds/and fish
don't know a thing about no hog behavior/*where's
the dynamite?*
I say you know/I say
you know.
And so do I.

What Would I Do White?

What would I do white?
What would I do clearly full
of not exactly beans nor
pearls my nose a manicure
my eyes a picture of your wall?

I would disturb the streets by
passing by so pretty kids
on stolen petty cash would look
at me like foreign
writing in the sky
I would forget my furs on any chair.
I would ignore the doormen at the knob
the social sanskrit of my life
unwilling to disclose my cosmetology,
I would forget.

Over my wine I would acquire
I would inspire big returns to equity
the equity of capital I am
accustomed to accept

like wintertime.

I would do nothing.
That would be enough.

In Memoriam:
Martin Luther King, Jr.

I
honey people murder mercy U.S.A.
the milkland turn to monsters teach
to kill to violate pull down destroy
the weakly freedom growing fruit
from being born

America

tomorrow yesterday rip rape
exacerbate despoil disfigure
crazy running threat the
deadly thrall
appall belief dispel
the wildlife burn the breast
the onward tongue
the outward hand
deform the normal rainy
riot sunshine shelter wreck
of darkness derogate
delimit blank
explode deprive
assassinate and batten up
like bullets fatten up
the raving greed
reactivate a springtime
terrorizing

death by men by more
than you or I can

STOP

II
They sleep who know a regulated place
or pulse or tide or changing sky
according to some universal
stage direction obvious
like shorewashed shells

we share an afternoon of mourning
in between no next predictable
except for wild reversal hearse rehearsal
bleach the blacklong lunging
ritual of fright insanity and more
deplorable abortion
more and
more

For Michael Angelo Thompson
(October 25, 1959–March 23, 1973)

So Brooklyn has become a holy place

the streets have turned to meadowland
where
wild
free
ponies
eat among the wild
free
flowers
growing there

                      Please do not forget.

A tiger does not fall or stumble
broken by an accident
A tiger does not lose his stride or
clumsy
slip and slide to tragedy
that buzzards feast upon.

                      Do not forget.

The Black prince Michael Black boy
our young brother
has not "died"
he
has not "passed away"

the Black prince Michael Black boy

our young brother

                  He was killed.
                  He did not die.

It was the city took him off
(that city bus)
and smashed him suddenly
to death
deliberate.

It was the city took him off
the hospital
that turned him down the hospital
that turned away from so much beauty
bleeding
bleeding
in Black struggle
                  just to live.
It was the city took him off
the casket names and faces
of the hatred spirit
stripped the force the
laughter and the agile power
of the child

                  He did not die.
                  A tiger does not fall.
                  Do not forget.

The streets have turned to meadowland
where
wild
free
ponies
eat among the wild
free
flowers
growing there

and Brooklyn
has become a holy place.

On Moral Leadership as a Political Dilemma
(Watergate, 1973)

I don't know why but
I cannot tell a lie

I chopped down the cherry tree
I did
I did that
yessirree
I chopped down the cherry tree

and to tell you the truth
see
that was only in the morning

which left a whole day and part
of an evening (until suppertime)
to continue doing what I like to do
about cherry trees

which is

to chop them down

then pick the cherries
and roll them into a cherry-pie circle
and then
stomp the cherries
stomp them
jumping up and down

hard and heavy
jumping up to stomp them
so the flesh leaks and the juice
runs loose
and then I get to pick at the pits
or else I pick up the cherry pits
(depending on my mood)
and then
I fill my mouth completely full
of cherry pits
and run over to the river

the Potomac
where I spit
the cherry pits
47 to 65 cherry pits spit
into the Potomac
at one spit

and to tell you the truth some more
if I ever see a cherry tree
standing around no matter where
and here let me please be perfectly clear
no matter where
I see a cherry tree
standing around
even if it belongs to a middle-American of
moderate means with a two-car family
that is falling apart in a respectable
civilized
falling apart
mind-your-manners manner

even then
or even if you happen to be
corporate rich or
unspeakably poor or famous
or fashionably thin or comfortably fat
or even as peculiar as misguided as
a Democrat

or even a Democrat

even then
see
if you have a cherry tree
and I see it
I will chop that cherry tree down
stomp the cherries
fill my mouth completely with the pits to
spit them into the Potomac
and I don't know why
it is
that I cannot tell a lie

but that's the truth.

Uhuru *in the O.R.*

The only successful heart transplant, of the first five attempts, meant that a black heart kept alive a white man—a white man who upheld apartheid.

I like love anonymous
more than murder incorporated or
shall we say South Africa
I like the Valentine the heart the power
incorruptible but failing body
flowers of the world

From my death the white man
takes new breath he stands as
formerly he stood and he commands me
for his good he overlooks
my land my people
in transition transplantations
hearts   and power
beating beating beating beating
hearts in transplantation
power in transition

If You Saw a Negro Lady

If you saw a Negro lady
sitting on a Tuesday
near the whirl-sludge doors of
Horn & Hardart on the main drag
of downtown Brooklyn

solitary and conspicuous as plain
and neat as walls impossible to
fresco and you watched her self-
conscious features shape about
a Horn & Hardart teaspoon
with a pucker from a cartoon

she would not understand
with spine as straight and solid
as her years of bending over floors
allowed

skin cleared of interest by a ruthless
soap   nails square and yellowclean
from metal files

sitting in a forty-year-old-flush
of solitude and prickling
from the new white cotton blouse
concealing nothing she had ever noticed
even when she bathed and never
hummed a bathtub tune nor knew one

If you saw her square
above the dirty
mopped-on antiseptic floors
before the rag-wiped table tops

little finger   broad and stiff
in heavy emulation of a cockney
mannerism
would you turn her treat
into surprise
observing

happy birthday

Roman Poem Number Five
For Millen and for Julius
and for Peter and for Eddie

1
This is a trip that strangers make
a journey ending on the beach where things
come together like four fingers on his
rather predictable

spine exposed by stars and
when he said this
has never happened before he
meant something
specific to himself because he could not
meet me anywhere inside but
you know
we were both out of the water
both out of it
and really what we wanted was
to screw ourselves into
the place

Pompeii
the Sarno River to the south
the mountain of Vesuvius to the north
the river did not burn
none of the records indicate
a burning river

        of all that went before the earth
        remembers nothing

                everywhere you see
        the fertility of its contempt
        the sweet alyssum blooming
        in the tomb

        an inward town
well suited to the lives
unraveled and undone
despite the secretly coloring
interior of their suddenly blasted
walls

Vesuvius created and destroyed
                WHOLE TOP OF THE
                    MOUNTAIN
                BLOWN OFF
                you can hum some words
                catchy like the title of a song
                (a little song)

WHOLE TOP OF THE
MOUNTAIN
BLOWN OFF
>(play it again
>sam)

Pompeii
the mountain truly coming to the men
who used to walk these streets these
sewer drains (the difference is
not very clear)

>juniper and cypress trees
>inspire the dark the only definite the trying
>forms on the horizon sky and sea and the Bay
>of Naples
>single trees
>against abstraction
>trees

the mainstreet moves directly
to the mouth the mountaintop
a vicious puckering

>This is a place where all the lives
>are planted in the ground
>the green things grow
>the other ones
>volcanic victims of an overflow
>a fireflushing tremble
>soul unseasonal
>in rush and rapture
>well they do not grow
>they seed the rest of us
>who prowl
>with plundersucking polysyllables
>to rape the corpse
>to fuck the fallen down and died
>long time ago
>again

his hand removes some of the sand on my neck
with difficulty

>did the river did the river burn

Pliny the Younger who delivered the volcano
who arrested the eruption into words
excited arrogant terrific
an exclusive
elegant account of mass destruction
79 A.D. that Johnny-on-the-spot say nothing
much about the river and
but eighteen is not too old to worry
for the rivers of the world
                                around the apple flesh and fit

loves holds easily
the hard skin soft enough

                      picture him sweet but cold
                      above the eyebrows
                      just a teenage witness with his pencil
                      writing down disaster

some say
put that apple into uniform
the tree itself wears buttons
in the spring
    VISITING DISASTER IS A WEIRD IDEA
    WHETHER YOU THINK ABOUT IT OR
    NOT

for example limestone the facade the statues the limestone statues of the everyone of them dead and dead and dead and no more face among the buried under twenty-seven feet of limestone other various in general all kinds of dust covering the dead the finally comfortable statues of the dusty smell today the nectar fragrance the sun knocks down my meter taking notes the wheel ruts gutter drains the overhanging upperstories the timber superstructure the dead the very dead the very very dead dead farmland pasture dead potato chip dead rooms of the dead the no longer turbulent blazing the no longer glorious inglorious the finish of the limestone building limestone statues look at the wild morninglories red and yellow laughter at the dying who dig into the death of limestone hard to believe the guide leads people to the public baths I Bagni di Publicci to talk about slaves and masters and how many sat at table he explains the plumbing where men bathed and where the women (bathed) hot water cold where the wall has a hole in it or where there is no hole in the wall and the tourists listening and

nobody asks him a question how about the living and the dead how
about that

Pompeii
and we are people who notice the mosaic decorations
of a coffin

we claim to be ordinary men and women or
extraordinary
elbows touching
cameras ready
sensible shoes
architects archaeologists classical
scholars one poet
Black and White and Jewish and Gentile and partly young
and married and once or twice married but
why do we follow
all
inquisitive
confessional or
necrophilomaniac or anyhow
alone
I am not here for you and I will stay there
we are disturbing the peace of the graveyard and
that is the believable limit of our impact
our intent
no
tonight he will hold me hard on the rocks of the ground
if the weather is warm and if
it doesn't rain

2
KEEP MOVING KEEP MOVING

the past is practically
behind us

half skull and teeth
knocked down running an
extreme tilt jerk tilted skull
stiff on its pole plaster cartilage
the legs apart like elbows
then the arms themselves the mouth

of the dead man tense defending still
the visitors peruse these plaster
memories of people
forms created in the cinders
living visitors admire the poise
of agony the poise of agony is
absolute
and who would call it sculpture
raise your own hand to the fire

> IN THE VILLA DEI
> MISTERI
> THERE ARE BLACK
> WALLS

another plaster person
crouched into his suffocation

yes well in the 14th century B.C.
they had this remarkable
bedroom where
they would keep one bed
or (some authorities say)
two beds
maybe it was the 15th

> Pompeii
> the unfamiliar plain
> the unfamiliar guilt
> annihilated men and women who
> most likely
> never heard of archaeology of
> dusty lust

all the possible homes were never built
(repeat)
"What's that?"

"That's a whorehouse, honey."

freckle hands chafing together
urbane
he tells the group that in
the declinium

women stayed apart with their loom
(in the declinium

occasional among the rocks the buttercups
obscure until the devil of the land)

> Perhaps Aristotle said the size
> of a city
> should take a man's shout to ears
> even on the edge
> but size never took anything
> much no matter what the porno
> makes believe but
> what will take in the
> scream of a what will
> take it in?

current calculations postulate the
human beings half the size of the market
place

> BEES
> LIZARDS

walls plus walls inhibit action on the lateral
or
with all them walls now how
you gone get next to me

> the falling of ashes
> the rolling lava

the way the things be happening
that garden story figleaf it belong
on top your head

> they had these industries these
> wool and fish sauce
> ways to spend the
> fooler
>
> even the moon is dark among us
> except for the lights by the mountainside
> except for the lights

20,000 people
subject
to Vesuvius in natural violence blew
up the handicrafted
fortress spirit of Pompeii
the liquid mangling
motley blood and lava
subject
20,000 people

KEEP MOVING KEEP MOVING

to them the theatre was "indispensable"
seats for 5,000 fabulous acoustics
what
was the performance of the people
in surprise
the rhythm chorus speaking
rescue
multitudes to acrobat survival
one last action on that last
entire stage
        today the cypress tree tips dally
        wild above the bleachers

when it happened what is happening to us
to hell with this
look at the vegetables blue
in the moonlight

              a pinetree colonnade
              the wall just under
              and the one man made

come to Pompeii
touch my tongue with yours
study the cold formulation of a fearful fix
grid patterns to the streets
the boundaries "unalterable"

the rights of property in stone
the trapezoidal plot the signals
of possession

        laughter
        (let's hear it loud)
        the laughing of the lava
        tell me
        stern
        rigid
        corpulent
        stories

the mountains surround the wastebasket bricks of our inquiry

in part
the waters barely stir with poison or with fish

        I think I know
        the people who
        were here
        where I am

3
my love completely and
one evening anywhere
I will arrive
the right way
given
up to you
and keep no peace
my body sings the force
of your disturbing legs

        WHAT DID YOU SAY?
        NO THANKS.
        WHAT DID YOU SAY?

Vesuvius
when Daddy Adam did what he did
the blame the bliss beginning
of no thanks
this is a bad connection
are you serious?

        the river did not burn

the group goes on
among the bones we travel

light into a new
starvation

                Pompeii was yesterday
here is Herculaneum
a second interesting testimony
to excuse me but how
will you try to give testimony
to a mountain?

                there it is baby there it is
                FURTHER EXCAVATION INTO
                HERCULANEUM
                ARRESTED TODAY BY RESSINI living
                inhabitants impoverished the non-
                descript Ressini town on top the
                ruins of

amazing Herculaneum
constructed on an earlier rehearsal flow
of lava maybe
courage or like that a seashore
a resort the remnant spread the
houses under houses
tall trees underlying grass the
pine and palm trees spring toward
Ressini grass retaining walls against the water
where there is no water and the sound of children
crying from which city is it Ressini is it
Herculaneum that
does not matter does it is it
the living or the visited the living or
the honored ERCOLANO

                SUCK
                SUCK HARD

"Here's where they sold spaghetti"
the leafy sound the feel
of the floor the tile
the painting of a wineglass
a wineglass on the wall unprecedented
turquoise colors would
the red walls make you warm
in winter

> INFORMATION
> WAS
> NOT AVAILABLE
> THE POOR
> OF RESSINI
> REFUSE
> TO COOPERATE
> WITH AUTHORITIES

you better watch out
next summer
and Ressini gone slide

> down inside them fancy
> stones
> and stay there
> using
> flashlight
> or whatever

NOBODY BUDGE
KEEP MOVING KEEP MOVING

> *cabbages cauliflower broccoli*
> the luminous leaves on the land

4
yesterday and yesterday
Paestum dates from four
hundred fifty years before the Christ
a fertile lowland calmly naked
and the sky excites the rubble flowers
in between
the mountains and the water
bleaching gentle
in the Middle Ages
mountainstreams came down
and made the meadow into marsh
marble travertine deposits when
the mountains left the land
the memory
deranged the water
turned the plants
to stone

this is the truth the people left this place alone

                      we are somewhere wounded by the wind
                      a mystery
                      a stand deserted by the trees

drizzling rain
destroys the dandelion
and your lips enlarge the glittering
of silence

        Paestum dedicated temples dedicated
        to the terra cotta figurines of trust
        the women in becoming mother of the world
        the midwives hold her arms
        like wings

the river does not burn

        delivering the life

the temple does not stand
still

        PERMISSION GRANTED TO PRESENT
        STONE SEX THE ECSTASY OF
        PAESTUM

4 main rows of
six in front
the tapering the girth the groove
the massive lifted fit of things
the penis worshiping
fecundity
fecundity
the crepis
stylobate
the cella
columns in entasis
magic
diminution
Doric
flutes
entablature
the leaning

curvilinear
the curve
the profile
magic
elasticity
diameter
effacement

THE TEMPLE IS THE COLOR OF A LIFE

>   ON STONE THE SUN CONTINUES
>   BLISTERING THE SURFACE
>   TENDERLY

>   WHAT TIME IS IT?

as we approach each other
someone else is making
a movie
there are horses
one or two beautiful men
and
birds flying
away

Roman Poem Number Six

You walk downstairs
to see this man who moves so
quietly in a dark room
where there are balancing
scales on every table.
Signore D'Ettore can tell
you anything about
communications if you mean
the weight the price
of letters
packages
and special post cards.

Hunch-back
short
his grey hair always groomed
meticulous
with a comb and just a touch
of grease
        for three months
he has worn the same well
tailored suit
a grey suit quite unlike
his hair.
        I find it restful
just to watch him making
judgements all of us accept.
"But are you sad?", he asks
me looking up.

"The world is beautiful
but men are bad," he says in
slow Italian.
I smile with him but still the problem
is not solved.
The photographs of Rome
must reach my father but the big
official looking book seems blank
the finger-nail of Signore D'Ettore
seems blind and wandering
from line to line among the countries
of a long
small-printed list.
"Jamaica? Where is Jamaica?"
I am silent. My Italian
is not good enough to say, "Jamaica
is an island where you can find
calypso roses sunlight and an old man
my father
on his knees."

About Enrique's Drawing

She lies down a mess
on white paper under glass
a long and a short leg a twisted
arm one good and even
muscular
an okay head
but body in a bloat
impossible

    "NO! Not impossible," he says
      standing.
    "It is
        a body.
    It is
        a structure
            that   is not
                    regular.
                    Do you see?
                          No?

    Listen:
        ONE
        ONE
        ONE TWO
        THREE FOUR
        ONE
        ONE
        ONETWOTHREE
        ONETWOTHREE
        ONE TWO
        ONETWOTHREE
        ONE TWO
        THREE FOUR
        ONE
        ONE...."

Enrique's body
has become the structure
of a dance. He is real.
And she

the woman lying down a mess
she
has become
mysterious.

On Declining Values

In the shadows of the waiting room
are other shadows
beaten
elderly women or
oldfolk bums
depending on your point of view

but
all depending

formerly mothers formerly wives
formerly citizens of some acceptable
position
but
depending and
depending
now exposed unable and unwashed
a slow and feeble crawling through the city
varicose
veins bulging
while the arteries the intake systems
harden
wither
shrivel
close
depending and depending

II
She will leave Grand Central Station
and
depending
spend two hours in St. Patrick's

if the guards there
if police ignore the grovelling length
of time it takes
a hungry woman
just to pray

but here
she whispers
with an aging boyfriend
fugitive and darkblue suited out
for begging who
has promised her a piece
of candy or an orange or an apple
if
they meet tomorrow
if the cops don't chase them separated
wandering under thin
gray hair

III
meanwhile
cops come quick
knockbopping up the oakwood benches
BANG
BOP
"GET OUTAHERE," they shout around
the ladies women sisters dying old and all
the formerly wives and mothers
shuffle soft
away
with paper shopping bags beside them
almost empty
and a medium young man
comes up
to ask a question:
"Tell me, I mean, seriously,
how does it feel to be beautiful?"

And I look back at him
a little bit alarmed
a little bit amused
before I say:

"It all depends too much
on you."

Some People

Some people despise me be-
cause I have a Venus mound
and not a penis

Does that *sound*
right
to you?

Fragments from a Parable
*Paul was Saul. Saul got on the road and the road
and somebody else changed him into somebody else
on the road.*

The worst is not knowing if I do take somebody's
word on it means I don't know and you have to believe
if you just don't know. How do I dare to stand as
still as I am still standing? Arrows create me.
And I despise directions. I am no wish.
After all the lunging still
myself is no sanctuary
birds feed and fly inside me shattering
the sullen spell of my desiring and the
accidental conquest.
Eyeless wings will
twist and sting
the tree of my remaining
like the wind.
Always there is not knowing, not knowing everything
of myself and having to take whoever you are at your
word. About me.

I am she.

And this is my story of Her. The story is properly yours to tell. You have created Her, but carelessly. As large as a person, she nevertheless learns why she walks and the aim of her gaze and the force of her breath from you who coax her to solve independently the mystery of your making: Her self.

Your patterns deny parenthood; deny every connection suggesting a connection; a consequence. She cannot discover how she began nor how she may begin. She seeks the authority of birth. Her fails.

Launched or spinning politely she fails to become her as self unless you allow her a specialty she will accept as her reason for being. Perhaps you allow her a skill like mercy or torment. The particular means nothing. Your approval matters like life and death. She is who I am.

I am.

My name is me. I am what you call black. (Only I am still. Arrest me. Arrest me any one or thing. If you arrest me I am yours. I am yours ready for murder or am I yours ready to expose any closed vein. Which is not important. Am I matter to you? Does it? You will try when. But now I am never under arrest. Meanwhile that slit allows me concentration on the bricks black between the windows. I am one of those suffering frozen to the perpetual corrosion of me. Where is the stillness that means?)

Here am I holding a pen with two fingers of frenzy of stream of retreat of connection and neurons. Supposedly there is a synapse between things like this: A difference:

between
beyond
beneath

illusions

At least a space without pulse. Without illusion: Only I am still: Only I am remaining. I repeat: I am not still: I repeat: Arrest me! You would say mine is a monotone if I could keep my tongue in my fist and my fist in my mouth and my mouth in a glass and that glass in my eyes. But monotony resonates: That would prove how merely am i a complicated position. Or riveted respectably with foot to the ground ignoring the drum and the furnace, the seeds and the water then could I say I am still pretending to be still.

But that complicated position is not. I was simply conceived by something like love. I was simply conceived during the war. My mother was the most beautiful woman in the world. My father was a macrosperm of lust for that woman painfully asleep on the battlefield. This lust, this loving uncertainty seized three hundred soldiers who paused at her silence as she lay. They made their rabid inquiry and left her.

For almost a year she wandered. For almost a year she wandered with a great song of hatred troubling her lips. She became deranged, an idiot, and everyone adored my mother. Certainly, her song amused them.

At last she struggled to be rid of me. Among the minerals she lay. Silently among the stones of sand she lay. There where the waters begin, like the most elemental mammal she lay. She lay down alone: a small whale. And at the impossible poise between absolute flux and accidental suspense, the most beautiful woman in the world became my mother. But as nothing is absolute nor accidental: I only exchanged equilibria: I was not particularly born.

For days I suckled on the blood of my delivery. Later she learned to ease her breasts and civilized my mouth with milk. No. I played with porpoises. No. Already there is progress. So. Not even then. Not even when beginning. Then is it the beginning not the stillness that means.

If I could eclipse the commencement of the moon. Skip the schedule. Be lunatic and always plunging. Then would I evade the agony of origin. Nor would I suffer an initiation. I would be just an actress, automatic to an action. And that must be how easy. The streets seem mine if I merge with a motion I do not determine. (The fireman slides down a pole. Yes and a siren controls him. There are no obstacle. He attaches himself to the vehicle carrying him. He follows the rules and there are rules how to approach a fire.)

But this is the matter of one step. If I pretend a paralysis am i not seeing? Am I not seeing white cranes idle tonight on the disappearing sidewalk, an empty truck tapered to a spoon that makes the sidewalk disappear, hatchet grass that punctures the pavement, careless carpentry to conceal an incomplete facade, a stairway almost destroyed? But I have reached this random excrement and already my eyes begin a building here at this place of pretended paralysis.

I AM NOT STILL AS i stand here like a phony catatonic:
aggressively resisting. I am not, it is not important
am i an impermeable membrane. This resistance
provokes the madness of enumeration:
   I am insensible to a,b,c,d,e,f,g,—
And the gamble of elimination:
$$A^x, B^x, C^x—.$$
The energy this resistance requires is itself an
alteration of temperature, at least.
So I surrender. I surrender and I multiply:
Polyblot:

Sponge.

Now am I leaning on a lamppost with metal leaves and a foundation of dung. Details obliterate within this lift. But I become corpuscular. I AM SEEKING THE CAPITAL INTRODUCTION TO THE VERY FIRST WORD OF MY MIND. I WANT TO DESTROY IT. I KNOW THAT THE VERY LAST WORD IS NOT ME.

But I am this moment and corpuscular. I am that horizontal line laughing at the bottom of the wall.
I might be the palace protected by the wall. But I refuse protection: I am better laughing at the bottom of the wall.

Within this kingdom of the wall is there a king and a palace gullible to light; gullibility to light despite the infinite opacities of active men opaque and infinite within this kingdom of the wall.
The forced stones spread. The town begins to grow among the bones.

My father came to sanctify my birth; to sanctify the birth of Her. He came to name my mother, His. He came to tame my mother and to shelter her. I am supposing.

We will stabilize the sand, he said. We will contain the waters. We will close the sky. We will squeeze the wind, he said.
   Build me a wall!
he said that.

He said: We will call this construction by a holy name. The syllable almost subdued him but he mastered his invention: masterfully then he said: The House.
My mother was His. The proud scheme of protection completely

included her. And it was only after he had protected my mother from experience that he became afraid of the experience of living with her labyrinthine illusions. Soon he seldom stayed in what he called The House.

At first such room as he created strangulated us. Then my mother began to vanish: security is not a color. Paralysis is not an exercise.

I was learning my father. My father was innocent perhaps: He wanted me to participate in his perseveration of himself: he wanted me to pursue the circle of his escape. And so I left The House and went to walk with him to what he called *the corner of The Wall.*

In that crude culmination, there where the exploitation of silence looks a cobweb, he taught me the way of The Wall.

Worship this thing, he said. Esteem this enemy of impulse. Let the wall become a sacred system for you, the fundamental lie you will believe.

Outside, inside, against, beside The Wall you will hover or hide, or climb, or penetrate, or withdraw. Whatever you choose, your deed will blunder as a dumb show on THE WALL. The absurd, insensible, arbitrary, obstacle qualities of The Wall will annihilate your mind. In this place of The Wall you will discover no necessity to act. The immoveable of your awareness is The Wall. You and what you do are optional. That is the secret, he said, that is the secret of your tragic spontaneity. Be glad you are optional, he told me. His voice was deep. His eyes were shut.

But here am I. Not there. Where am I is there where I am. Here am I. Am I there where nothing is here where nothing is NOW? *I am not here for you and I will stay there.* Now there is nothing but now which is why am I here?

    Look at the cloud on the circle.
    I am full suddenly full of light.

My father said: There shall be shadow.
    I am shining shadows on The Wall.
And my father was only a shadow. His shadow of flesh divulged me: I was an apology of bone.

Anyone is of no consequence. How am I my one?

If I am, I am If in the middle of The Way. The Way leads neither north nor south with possibilities.
Possibilities preclude a wall.
The Way lies in between two walls.

These are the ways of first and last reality. These are the ways of populous, foul, vertiginous, predatory, vicious, liquidating, lavatory truth. The Way is not a transformative via, nor a road for flight from arrival nor the rhythmic gesture of a street. The Way reveals only the curb.

It is an intestinal trap: a trick coiled labyrinthine and gutteral. I am in the middle of the way.

I am in the middle of a dirty line squeezed by bricks of the wall precluding possibility. But I am not if I am in the middle clearly. If I am clearly then am I in the way of nothing.

But I am not alive nor dead.

I am not alive nor dead nor gray nor anything absolute but I am black. That may mean gamma rays or brown or turd is another word that may mean brown inside this intestinal trap. Brown may mean negro. Negro may mean nothing. I am in the middle of delusion. I am in the way of nothing. But I am in the way.

My father loved the delusion he sired. The fundamental dream of my mother, her unnatural ignorance refreshed him and he surrounded her with new unnecessaries; things that do not matter, have no matter like The Wall. He gave to her. He gave of himself to her. He gave gold to her. He told her stories of herself. He told her the myth of the mirror. He made her the mirror of myth. He said to my mother many nouns. He said face and sky and ear and emerald and eye, but then he said grass. He said she was grass.

My mother wondered what she was. And so he opened the house.
He gave evening to her and winter.
He gave her alternative illusions.
He gave her a glimpse of endless, enjoyable illusion.
My father opened the house with windows.

I asked my father where was grass Or is there more than my mother as a metaphor. Around me was my mother and The Wall and the words my father used to call her as a sound
    I asked my father is there no grass in The House

While we live in The House he said there is no grass
When you have done with living in The House then
when you leave the Wall
when you stop your self
people carry you over THE WALL and bury you under the grass

Sometimes my father said smiling at me sometimes people bury you under the grass and near an evergreen tree

I was happy to think of the burial place and I asked my father to tell me a word for my first dream

He held me on his lap as he gave me the word for my dream *Cemetery* was what he whispered in my ear.

I would like to live in that cemetery of trees and grass but he told me I must go with him struggling for survival until I finally have done with living in The House

Then will I be taken to the cemetery And this my father called A Promise

> gulls fly along a shoulder
> I am baffled by
> your neck concealing
> flight

It does not do to say it. And I would not but I cannot do. You will not let me more than words. I wish that this word were less than. I. I will to be more than this word. You will laughing let me try. For example, flight.

Three million molecules and marrow but still I will not rise and am I still. But is there that word. Desire has its sound but is there a stillness that means. There are wings between my teeth. Or my mouth consumes some cumulae fuming near my eyes striated from the hours of the day or garbanzo is a chick-pea. Still I am still.

Touch my tongue with yours.

I would swallow the limbs of your body and refuse to Write Down and disturb the magic of my engorgement

Let me more than words: I would be more than medium or limestone. I would be more than looking more than knowing more than any of these less than looking less than knowing (*words*)

On the dirt and stones between us was my hand that lay between us like a word between my eyes

On the dirt and stones between us was my hand that lay between us like another stone. Desire has no sound.

I looked the length of more than light at you away from me Things were hanging   Rosebush maid and mirror hung. Wires screws hooks and rope were there   Rope no longer green is there in that very long room

I have heard the rope of your throat
I have heard the rope in your throat ready to squeeze
me into the syntax of stone
The sound of my life is a name you may not remember
I am losing the touch of the world to a word
You must have said anything to me

                                            Written from 1958 to 1973

PART TWO

FROM
Passion

For the Sake of a People's Poetry:
Walt Whitman and the Rest of Us

In America, the father is white: It is he who inaugurated the experiment of this republic. It is he who sailed his way into slave ownership. It is he who availed himself of my mother: the African woman whose function was miserably defined by his desirings, or his rage. It is he who continues to dominate the destiny of the Mississippi River, the Blue Ridge Mountains, and the life of my son. Understandably, then, I am curious about this man.

Most of the time my interest can be characterized as wary, at best. Other times, it is the interest a pedestrian feels for the fast-traveling truck about to smash into him. Or her. Again. And at other times it is the curiosity of a stranger trying to figure out the system of the language that excludes her name and all of the names of all of her people. It is this last that leads me to the poet Walt Whitman.

Trying to understand the system responsible for every boring, inaccessible, irrelevant, derivative, and pretentious poem that is glued to the marrow of required readings in American classrooms, or trying to understand the system responsible for the exclusion of every hilarious, amazing, visionary, pertinent, and unforgettable poet from N.E.A. grants and from national publications, I come back to Walt Whitman.

What in the hell happened to him? Wasn't he a white man? Wasn't he some kind of a father to American literature? Didn't he talk about this New World? Didn't he see it? Didn't he sing this New World, this America, on a New World, an American scale of his own visionary invention?

It so happens that Walt Whitman is the one white father who shares the systematic disadvantages of his heterogeneous offspring trapped inside a closet that is, in reality, as huge as the continental spread of North and South America. What Whitman envisioned we, the people and the poets of the New World, embody. He has been punished for the political meaning of his vision. We are being punished for the moral questions that our very lives provoke.

At home as a child I learned the poetry of the Bible and the poetry of Paul Laurence Dunbar. As a student, I diligently followed orthodox directions from *The Canterbury Tales* right through *The Waste Land* by that consummate Anglophile whose name I can never remember. And I kept waiting. It was, I thought, all right to deal with daffodils in the seventeenth century on an island as much like Manhattan as I resemble

Queen Mary. But what about Dunbar? When was he coming up again? And where were the Black poets altogether? And who were the women poets I might reasonably emulate? And wasn't there, ever, a great poet who was crazy about Brooklyn or furious about war? And I kept waiting. And I kept writing my own poetry. And I kept reading apparently underground poetry: poetry kept strictly off campus. And I kept reading the poetry of so many gifted students when I became a teacher myself, and I kept listening to the wonderful poetry of the multiplying numbers of my friends who were and who are New World poets until I knew, for a fact, that there was and that there is an American, a New World, poetry that is as personal, as public, as irresistible, as quick, as necessary, as unprecedented, as representative, as exalted, as speakably commonplace, and as musical, as an emergency phone call.

But I didn't know about Walt Whitman. Yes: I had heard about this bohemian, this homosexual even, who wrote something about The Captain and The Lilacs, but nobody ever told me he was crucial to a native American literature. Not only was Whitman not required reading, in the sense that Wordsworth and Robert Herrick are required reading, he was, on the contrary, presented as a rather hairy buffoon suffering from a childish proclivity for exercise and open air. Nevertheless, it is through the study of all the poems and all the ideas of this particular white father that I have reached a tactical, if not strategic, understanding of the racist, sexist, and anti-American predicament that condemns most New World writing to peripheral/small press/unpublished manuscript status.

Before these United States, the great poems of the world earned their luster through undeniable forms of spontaneous popularity: Generations of a people chose to memorize and then to further elaborate and then to impart these songs to the next generation. I am talking about people: African families and Greek families and the families of the Hebrew tribes and all that multitude to whom the Bhagavad-Gita is as daily as the sun. If these poems were not always religious, they were certainly moral in motive, or in accomplishment, or both. None of these great poems could be mistaken for the poetry of another country, another time; you do not find a single helicopter taking off or landing in any of the sonnets of Elizabethan England, nor do you run across Jamaican rice and peas in any of the psalms. Evidently, one criterion for great poetry used to be the requirements of cultural nationalism.

But with the advent of the 36-year-old poet Walt Whitman, the phenomenon of a people's poetry, or great poetry and its spontaneous popularity, could no longer be assumed. The physical immensity and the far-flung population of this New World decisively separated the poet from the suitable means to produce and to distribute his poetry. Now there would have to be intermediaries—critics and publishers—whose marketplace principles of scarcity would, logically, oppose them to populist traditions of art. In place of the democratic concepts, elitist Old World concepts would, logically, govern their policies; in the context of such considerations, an American literary establishment antithetical to the New World meanings of America took root. And this is one reason why the pre-eminently American white father of American poetry is practically unknown outside the realm of caricature and rumor in his own country.

As a matter of fact, if you hope to hear about Whitman, your best bet is to leave home: Ignore prevailing American criticism and, instead, ask anybody anywhere else in the world this question: As Shakespeare is to England, Dante to Italy, Tolstoi to Russia, Goethe to Germany, Agostinho Neto to Angola, Pablo Neruda to Chile, Mao Tse-tung to China, and Ho Chi Minh to Vietnam, who is the great American writer, the distinctively American poet, the giant American "literatus"? Undoubtedly, the answer will be *Walt Whitman.* He is the poet who wrote:

A man's body at auction,
(For before the war I often go to the slave-mart and watch the sale,)
I help the auctioneer, the sloven does not half know his business.

Gentlemen look on this wonder,
Whatever the bids of the bidders they cannot be high enough for it

"I Sing the Body Electric"

I ask you today: Who in America would publish those lines? They are all wrong! In the first place, there is nothing obscure, nothing contrived, noting an ordinary straphanger in the subway would be puzzled by. In the second place, the voice of those lines is intimate and direct at once: It is the voice of the poet who assumes that he speaks to an equal and that he need not fear that equality; on the contrary, the intimate distance between the poet and the reader is a distance that assumes there is everything important, between them, to be shared. And what is poetic about a line of words that runs as long as a regular, a spoken idea? You could more easily imagine an actual human being speaking such lines than you could imagine an artist composing them in a room carefully separated from other rooms of a house, carefully separated from other lives of a family: This can't be poetry. Besides, these lines apparently serve an expressly moral purpose! Then is this didactic/political writing? This cannot be good poetry. And, in fact, you will never see, for example, *The New Yorker* publishing a poem marked by such splendid deficiencies.

Consider the inevitable, the irresistible simplicity of that enormous moral idea:

Gentlemen look on this wonder,
Whatever the bids of the bidders they cannot be high enough for
    it . . .
This is not only one man, this the father of those who shall be
fathers in their turns,
In him the start of populous states and rich republics,
Of him countless immortal lives with countless embodiments and
    enjoyments.

"I Sing the Body Electric"

This is not an idea generally broadcast in America. It is an idea to violate the marketplace: The poet is trying to rescue a human being while even the poem cannot be saved from the insolence of marketplace evaluation!

Indeed Walt Whitman and the traceable descendants of Whitman, those who follow his democratic faith into obviously New World forms of experience and art, they suffer from the same establishment rejection and contempt that forced this archetypal American genius to publish, distribute, and review his own work—by himself. The descendants I have in mind include those unmistakably contemporaneous young poets who base themselves upon domesticities such as disco, Las Vegas, McDonald's, and forty-dollar running shoes. Also within the Whitman tradition, Black and Third World poets traceably transform, and further, the egalitarian sensibility that isolates that one white father from his more powerful compatriots. And I am thinking of those feminist poets who are evidently intent upon speaking with a maximal number and diversity of other American lives. And I am thinking of such first-rank heroes of the New World as Pablo Neruda and Agostinho Neto. Except for these last two, New World poets are overwhelmingly forced to publish their own works, or seek the commitment of a small press or else give it up entirely. That is to say, the only peoples who can test or verify the meaning of America as a democratic state, as a pluralistic culture, are the very peoples whose contribution to a national vision and discovery meet with general ridicule and disregard. A democratic state does not, after all, exist for the few, but for the many. A democratic state is not proven by the welfare of the strong but by the welfare of the weak. And unless that many, that manifold constitution of diverse peoples can be seen as integral to the national art/the national consciousness, you might as well mean only Czechoslovakia when you talk about the U.S.A., or only Ireland, or merely France, or exclusively white men.

The fate of Pablo Neruda differs from the other Whitman descendants because Neruda was born into a sovereign New World country where a majority of the citizens did not mistake themselves for Englishmen or long to find themselves struggling, at most, with cucumber sandwiches and tea. He was never European. His anguish was not aroused by three-piece suits and rolled umbrellas. When he cries, toward the conclusion of *The Heights of Macchu Picchu*, "Arise to birth with me, my brother," he plainly does not allude to Lord or Colonel Anybody At All. As he writes, earlier, in that amazing poem:

I came by another way, river by river, street after street,
city by city, one bed and another,
forcing the salt of my mask through a wilderness;
and there, in the shame of the ultimate hovels, lampless and fireless,
lacking bread or a stone or a stillness, alone in myself,
I whirled at my will, dying the death that was mine.

Of course Neruda has not escaped all of the untoward consequences common to Whitman descendants. American critics and translators never weary of asserting that Neruda is a quote great unquote poet despite the political commitment of his art and despite the artistic consequences of that commitment. Specifically, Neruda's self-conscious decision to write in a manner readily comprehensible to the masses of his countrymen and his self-conscious decision to specify outright the United Fruit Company when that was the instigating subject of his poem become unfortunate moments in an otherwise supposedly sublime, not to mention surrealist, deeply Old World and European but nonetheless Chilean case history. To assure the validity of this perspective, the usual American critic and translator presents you with a smattering of the unfortunate, ostensibly political poetry and, on the other hand, buries you under volumes of Neruda's early work that antedates the Spanish Civil War or, in other words, that antedates Neruda's serious conversion to a political world view.

This kind of artistically indefensible censorship would have you perceive chasmic and even irreconcilable qualitative differences between the poet who wrote:

You, my antagonist, in that splintering dream
like the bristling glass of gardens, like a menace
of ruinous bells, volleys
of blackening ivy at the perfume's center
enemy of the great hipbones my skin has touched
with a harrowing dew

"The Woes and the Furies"

and the poet who wrote, some twenty years later, these lines from the poem entitled "The Dictators":

lament was perpetual and fell, like a plant and its pollen,
forcing a lightless increase in the blinded, big leaves.
And bludgeon by bludgeon, on the terrible waters,
scale over scale in the bog,
the snout filled with silence and slime
and vendetta was born.

According to prevalent American criticism, that later poem by Neruda represents a lesser achievement precisely because it can be understood by more people, more easily, than the first. It is also denigrated because it attacks a keystone of the Old World, namely dictatorship, or, in other words, power and privilege for the few.

The peculiar North American vendetta against Walt Whitman, against the first son of this democratic union, should be further fathomed: Neruda's eminence is now acknowledged on international levels; his work profoundly affects many North American poets who do not realize, because they have never been shown, the North American/the Walt Whitman origins for so much that is singular and worthy in the poetry of Neruda. You will even find American critics who congratulate Neruda for overcoming the "Whitmanese" content of his art! This perfidious arrogance is as calculated as it is common. You cannot persuade anyone seriously familiar with Neruda's life and art that he could have found cause, at any point, to disagree with the tenets, the analysis, and the authentic New World vision presented by Walt Whitman in his essay "Democraic Vistas," which remains the most signal and persuasive manifesto of New World thinking and belief in print.

Let me define my terms in brief: New World does not mean New England. New World means non-European; it means new, it means big, it means heterogeneous, it means unknown, it means free, it means an end to feudalism, caste, privilege, and the violence of power. It means *wild* in the sense that a tree growing away from the earth enacts a wild event. It means *democratic* in the sense that, as Whitman wrote:

I believe a leaf of grass is no less than the journey-work of the
   stars . . .
And a mouse is miracle enough to stagger sextillions of infidels.

"Song of Myself"

New World means, in Whitman's words, "I keep as delicate around the bowels as around the head and heart." New World means, again, to quote Whitman, "By God! I will accept nothing which all cannot have their counterpart of on the same terms." In "Democratic Vistas," Whitman declared,

> As the greatest lessons of Nature through the universe are perhaps the lessons of variety and freedom, the same present the greatest lessons also in New World politics and progress . . . Sole among nationalities, these States have assumed the task to put in forms of history, power and practicality, on areas of amplitude rivaling the operations of the physical kosmos, the moral political speculations of ages, long, long deferr'd, the democratic republican principle, and the theory of development and perfection by voluntary standards, and self-reliance.

Listen to this white man; he is so weird! Here he is calling aloud for an American, a democratic spirit, an American, a democratic idea that could morally constrain and coordinate the material body of U.S.A. affluence and piratical outreach, more than a hundred years ago. He wrote:

The great poems, Shakespeare included, are poisonous to the idea of the pride and dignity of the common people, the lifeblood of democracy. The models of our literature, as we get it from other lands, ultra marine, have had their birth in courts, and bask'd and grown in castle sunshine; all smells of princes' favors . . . Do you call those genteel little creatures

American poets? Do you term that perpetual, pistareen, paste-pot work, American art, American drama, taste, verse?
... We see the sons and daughters of The New World, ignorant of its genius, not yet inaugurating the native, the universal, and the near, still importing the distant, the partial, the dead.

Abhorring the "thin sentiment of parlors, parasols, piano-song, tinkling rhymes," Whitman conjured up a poetry of America, a poetry of democracy that would not "mean the smooth walks, trimm'd hedges, poseys and nightingales of the English poets, but the whole orb, with its geologic history, the Kosmos, carrying fire and snow that rolls through the illimitable areas, light as a feather, though weighing billions of tons."

Well, what happened?

Whitman went ahead and wrote the poetry demanded by his vision. He became, by thousands upon thousands of words, a great America poet:

There was a child went forth every day,
And the first object he look'd upon, that object he became,
And that object became part of him for the day or a certain part
of the day,
Or for many years or stretching cycles of years.

The early lilacs became part of this child,
And grass and white and red morning-glories, and white and red
clover, and the song of the phoebe-bird,

"There Was a Child Went Forth"

And elsewhere he wrote:

It avails not, time nor place—distance avails not,
I am with you, you men and women of a generation, or ever so
many generations hence,
Just as you feel when you look on the river and sky, so I felt,
Just as any of you is one of a living crowd, I was one of a crowd,
Just as you are refresh'd by the gladness of the river and the bright
flow, I was refresh'd,
Just as you stand and lean
on the rail, yet hurry with the swift
current, I stood yet was hurried,

Just as you look on the numberless masts of ships and the thick-stemm'd pipes of steamboats,
I look'd . . .

"Crossing Brooklyn Ferry"

This great American poet of democracy as cosmos, this poet of a continent as consciousness, this poet of the many people as one people, this poet of a diction comprehensible to all, of a vision insisting on each, of a rhythm/a rhetorical momentum to transport the reader from the Brooklyn ferry into the hills of Alabama and back again, of line after line of bodily, concrete detail that constitutes the mysterious, the cellular tissues of a nation indivisible but dependent upon and astonishing in its diversity, this white father of a great poetry deprived of its spontaneous popularity/a great poetry hidden away from the ordinary people it celebrates so well, he has been, again and again, cast aside as an undisciplined poseur, a merely freak eruption of prolix perversities.

Last year, the *New York Times Book Review* saw fit to import a European self-appointed critic of American literature to address the question: Is there a great American poet? Since this visitor was ignorant of the philosophy and the achievements of Walt Whitman, the visitor, Denis Donoghue, comfortably excluded every possible descendant of Whitman from his erstwhile cerebrations: Only one woman was mentioned. (She, needless to add, did not qualify.) No poets under fifty, and not one Black or Third World poet, received even cursory assessment. Not one poet of distinctively New World values, and their formal embodiment, managed to dent the illiterate suavity of Donoghue's public display.

This *New York Times* event perpetuates American habits of beggarly, absurd deference to the Old World. And these habits bespeak more than marketplace intrusions into cultural realms: We erase ourselves through self-hatred, we lend our silence to the American anti-American process whereby anything and anyone special to this nation state becomes liable to condemnation because it is what it is, truly.

Against self-hatred there is Whitman and there are all of the New World poets who insistently devise legitimate varieties of cultural nationalism. There is Whitman and all of the poets whose lives have been baptized by witness to blood, by witness to cataclysmic, political confrontations from the Civil War through the Civil Rights Era, through the Women's Movement, and on and on through the conflicts between the hungry and the fat, the wasteful, the bullies.

In the poetry of The New World, you meet with a reverence for the material world that begins with a reverence for human life, an intellectual trust in sensuality as a means of knowledge and of unity, an easily deciphered system of reference, aspiration to a believable, collective voice and, consequently, emphatic preference for broadly accessible languae and/or "spoken" use of language, a structure of forward energies that interconnects apparently discrete or even conflictual elements, saturation by quotidian data, and a deliberate balancing of perception with vision: a balancing of sensory report with moral exhortation.

All of the traceable descendants of Whitman have met with an establishment, an academic, reception disgracefully identical: Except for the New World poets who live and write beyond the boundaries of the U.S.A., the offspring of this one white father encounter everlasting marketplace disparagement as crude or optional or simplistic or, as Whitman himself wrote, "hankering, gross, mystical, nude."

I too am a descendant of Walt Whitman. And I am not by myself struggling to tell the truth about this history of so much land and so much blood, of so much that should be sacred and so much that has been desecrated and annihilated boastfully.

My brothers and my sisters of this New World, we remember that, as Whitman said,

I do not trouble my spirit to vindicate itself or be understood,
I see that the elementary laws never apologize.

"Song of Myself"

We do not apologize because we are not Emily Dickinson, Ezra Pound, T. S. Eliot, Wallace Stevens, Robert Lowell, or Elizabeth Bishop. If we are nothing to them, to those who love them, they are nothing to us! Or, as Whitman exclaimed: "I exist as I am, that is enough."

New World poetry moves into and beyond the light of the lives of Walt Whitman, Pablo Neruda, Agostinho Neto, Gabriela Mistral, Langston Hughes, Margaret Walker, and Edward Brathwaite.

I follow this movement with my own life. I am calm and I am smiling as we go. Is it not written somewhere very near to me:

A man's body at auction . . .
Gentlemen, look on this wonder,
Whatever the bids of the bidders they cannot be high enough for it

And didn't that weird white father predict this truth that is always growing:

I swear to you the architects shall appear without fail,
I swear to you they will understand you and justify you,
The greatest among them shall be he who best knows you, and encloses all and is faithful to all,
He and the rest shall not forget you, they shall perceive that you are not an iota less than they,
You shall be fully glorified in them.

"A Song of the Rolling Earth"

Walt Whitman and all of the New World poets coming after him, we, too, go on singing this America.

*June Jordan
New York City 1979*

Current Events

He did not!
He did so!
He did not!
I'm telling you!
You lie!
Uh-unhh.
You're kidding me!
Cross my heart and hope to die!
Really?
No shit!
Yeah?
Yeah!
The What?
The Ayatollah Khomeini!
Getoutahere.
Square business!
The Who?
The Ayatollah Khomeini of Iran!
So?
So he said it!
Big deal.

That's what I'm saying:
Thursday
November 15th
1979
the headline reads:
IRAN SET TO
FREE WOMEN
AND BLACKS
Run that by, again!
Okay:
Thursday
November 15th
No! Not that part!
Just wait a second:
Thursday
November 15th
1979 and
this is the headline:
IRAN SET TO
FREE WOMEN
AND BLACKS:
See now
I told you it's a big deal!
How was I supposed to know?
Girl
you better keep up with the news!
Yeah, yeah:
I'm planning to!

Case in Point

A friend of mine who raised six daughters and
who never wrote what she regards as serious
until she
was fifty-three
tells me there is no silence peculiar
to the female

I have decided I have something to say
about female silence: so to speak
these are my 2¢ on the subject:

2 weeks ago I was raped for the second
time in my life the first occasion
being a whiteman and the most recent
situation being a blackman actually
head of the local NAACP

Today is 2 weeks after the fact
of that man straddling
his knees either side of my chest
his hairy arm and powerful left hand
forcing my arms and my hands over my head
flat to the pillow while he rammed
what he described as his quote big dick
unquote into my mouth
and shouted out: "D'ya want to swallow
my big dick; well, do ya?"

He was being rhetorical.
My silence was peculiar
to the female.

Newport Jazz Festival: Saratoga Springs and Especially about George Benson and everyone who was listening

We got to the point of balloons all of us
held aloft/a tender tapping at the skin
of coloring translucent
and
nothing was too deep but the incendiary/slow the rainy/
rainbow crowded surface did not keep
anybody from caring enough to undertake a random
openhanded sharing of much hefty
toke equipment/smoke
was passing by like kisses in the air
where little girls
blew bubbles
benedictory below the softly bloated
clouds

While the trumpets lifted sterling
curvilinear tonalities
to turn the leaves down low/well-
lit by glowing globes of candlelight
that man was singing
That man was singing
Baby
Baby if you come with me
I'll make you my own Dairy Queen
or if that's locked we'll find an all-night Jack-
in-the-Box steak sandwich/fried onion rings
blackcherry/strawberry/butterscotch/shake
blackcherry/strawberry/butterscotch
shake
blackcherry/strawberry/butterscotch
shake

Baby
if you come now Baby if you if you Baby if you come
now

Patricia's Poem

"Listen
after I have set the table
folded the scottowel into napkins
cooked this delicious eggplant stuffed
with bulghur wheat
then baked the whole thing under a careful
covering of mozzarella cheese
and
said my grace

don't you bring Anita Bryant/Richard
Pryor/the Justices of the Supreme Court/don't
you bring any of those people in here
to spoil my digestive processes
and ruin
my dinner

you hear?"

Letter to the Local Police

Dear Sirs:

I have been enjoying the law and order of our
community throughout the past three months since
my wife and I, our two cats, and miscellaneous
photographs of the six grandchildren belonging to
our previous neighbors (with whom we were very
close) arrived in Saratoga Springs which is clearly
prospering under your custody

Indeed, until yesterday afternoon and despite my
vigilant casting about, I have been unable to discover
a single instance of reasons for public-spirited concern,
much less complaint

You may easily appreciate, then, how it is that
I write to your office, at this date, with utmost
regret for the lamentable circumstances that force
my hand

Speaking directly to the issue of moment:

I have encountered a regular profusion of certain
unidentified roses, growing to no discernible purpose,
and according to no perceptible control, approximately
one quarter mile west of the Northway, on the southern
side

To be specific, there are practically thousands of
the aforementioned abiding in perpetual near riot
of wild behavior, indiscriminate coloring, and only
the Good Lord Himself can say what diverse soliciting
of promiscuous cross-fertilization

As I say, these roses, no matter what the apparent
background, training, tropistic tendencies, age,
or color, do not demonstrate the least inclination
toward categorization, specified allegiance, resolute
preference, consideration of the needs of others, nor
any other minimal traits of decency

May I point out that I did not assiduously seek out
this colony, as it were, and that these certain

unidentified roses remain open to viewing even by
children, with or without suitable supervision

(My wife asks me to append a note as regards the seasonal but
nevertheless seriously licentious
phenomenon of honeysuckle under the moon that one may
apprehend at the corner of Nelson and Main

However, I have recommended that she undertake direct
correspondence with you, as regards this: yet
another civic disturbance in our midst)

I am confident that you will devise and pursue
appropriate legal response to the roses in question
If I may aid your efforts in this respect, please
do not hesitate to call me into consultation

                                    Respectfully yours,

Poem about Police Violence

Tell me something
what you think would happen if
everytime they kill a black boy
then we kill a cop
everytime they kill a black man
then we kill a cop

you think the accident rate would lower
subsequently?

sometimes the feeling like amaze me baby
comes back to my mouth and I am quiet
like Olympian pools from the running the
mountainous snows under the sun

sometimes thinking about the 12th House of the Cosmos
or the way your ear ensnares the tip
of my tongue or signs that I have never seen
like DANGER WOMEN WORKING

I lose consciousness of ugly bestial rabid
and repetitive affront as when they tell me

18 cops in order to subdue one man
18 strangled him to death in the ensuing scuffle (don't
you idolize the diction of the powerful: *subdue* and
scuffle my oh my) and that the murder
that the killing of Arthur Miller on a Brooklyn
street was just a "justifiable accident" again
(again)

People been having accidents all over the globe
so long like that I reckon that the only
suitable insurance is a gun
I'm saying war is not to understand or rerun
war is to be fought and won

sometimes the feeling like amaze me baby
blots it out/the bestial but
not too often

tell me something
what you think would happen if
everytime they kill a black boy
then we kill a cop
everytime they kill a black man
then we kill a cop

you think the accident rate would lower
subsequently?

Sketching in the Transcendental

Through the long night the long trucks running the road

The wind in the white pines does not ululate like
that

Nor do the boreal meadowlands the mesopotamia
of the spirit does not sing

the song of the long trucks

The spirit differs
from a truck

a helluva lot

A Poem about Intelligence for My Brothers and Sisters

A few years back and they told me Black
means a hole where other folks
got brain/it was like the cells in the heads
of Black children was out to every hour on the hour naps
Scientists called the phenomenon the Notorious
Jensen Lapse, remember?
Anyway I was thinking
about how to devise
a test for the wise
like a Stanford-Binet
for the C.I.A.
you know?
Take Einstein
being the most the unquestionable the outstanding
the maximal mind of the century
right
And I'm struggling against this lapse leftover
from my Black childhood to fathom why
anybody should say so:
$E = mc\ squared$?
I try that on this old lady live on my block:
She sweeping away Saturday night from the stoop
and mad as can be because some absolute
jackass have left a kingsize mattress where
she have to sweep around it stains and all she
don't want to know nothing about in the first place
"Mrs. Johnson!" I say, leaning on the gate
between us: "What you think about somebody come up
with an E equals $M\ C\ 2$?"
"How you doin," she answer me, sideways, like she don't
want to let on she know I ain
combed my hair yet and here it is
Sunday morning but still I have the nerve
to be bothering serious work with these crazy
questions about
"E equals what you say again, dear?"
Then I tell her, "Well
also this same guy? I think

he was undisputed Father of the Atom Bomb!"
"That right." She mumbles or grumbles, not too politely
"And dint remember to wear socks when he put on
his shoes!" I add on (getting desperate)
at which point Mrs. Johnson take herself and her broom
a very big step down the stoop away from me
"And never did nothing for nobody in particular
lessen it was a committee
and
used to say, 'What time is it?'
and
you'd say, 'Six o'clock.'
and
he'd say, 'Day or night?'
and
and he never made nobody a cup a tea
in his whole brilliant life!"
"and
(my voice rises slightly)
and
he dint never boogie neither: never!"

"Well," say Mrs. Johnson, "Well, honey,
I do guess
that's genius for you."

1977: Poem for Mrs. Fannie Lou Hamer

You used to say, "June?
Honey when you come down here you
supposed to stay with me. Where
else?"
Meanin home
against the beer the shotguns and the
point of view of whitemen don'
never see Black anybodies without
some violent itch start up.
                    The ones who
said, "No Nigga's Votin in This Town . . .

lessen it be feet first to the booth"
Then jailed you
beat you brutal
bloody/battered/beat
you blue beyond the feeling
of the terrible

And failed to stop you.
Only God could but He
wouldn't stop
you
fortress from self-
pity

Humble as a woman anywhere
I remember finding you inside the laundromat
in Ruleville
    lion spine relaxed/hell
    what's the point to courage
    when you washin clothes?

But that took courage

    just to sit there/target
    to the killers lookin
    for your singin face
    perspirey through the rinse
    and spin

and later
you stood mighty in the door on James Street
loud callin:

    "BULLETS OR NO BULLETS!
    THE FOOD IS COOKED
    AN' GETTIN COLD!"

We ate
A family tremulous but fortified
by turnips/okra/handpicked
like the lilies

filled to the very living
full
one solid gospel
    (*sanctified*)

one gospel
> (*peace*)

one full Black lily
luminescent
in a homemade field

of love

Poem for South African Women
Commemoration of the 40,000 women and children who, August 9, 1956, presented themselves in bodily protest against the "dompass" in the capital of apartheid. Presented at The United Nations, August 9, 1978.

Our own shadows disappear as the feet of thousands
by the tens of thousands pound the fallow land
into new dust that
rising like a marvelous pollen will be
fertile
even as the first woman whispering
imagination to the trees around her made
for righteous fruit
from such deliberate defense of life
as no other still
will claim inferior to any other safety
in the world

The whispers too they
intimate to the inmost ear of every spirit
now aroused they
carousing in ferocious affirmation
of all peaceable and loving amplitude
sound a certainly unbounded heat
from a baptismal smoke where yes
there will be fire

And the babies cease alarm as mothers
raising arms
and heart high as the stars so far unseen

nevertheless hurl into the universe
a moving force
irreversible as light years
traveling to the open
eye

And who will join this standing up
and the ones who stood without sweet company
will sing and sing
back into the mountains and
if necessary
even under the sea

we are the ones we have been waiting for

Unemployment Monologue

You can call me Herbie Jr. or Ashamah
Kazaam. It don' matter much. The thing
is you don' wan' my name you
wanna mug shot
young
Black
male
who scares you chickenshit just
standin on the street just lookin
at you pass me by.
But I ain doin nothing I ain goin nowhere an
you
know it an
if you call me "Herbie" I don' mind
or "Junior"/that's all right
or "Ashamah Kazaam"/that's cool.
I say it don' really matter much
and then again/see
I may call you sweetmeat

I may call you tightass I might
one night I might break the windows
of the house you live in/I
might get tight and take your

wallet outasight/I might
hide out in the park to chase
you in the dark/etcetera/it
don' matter/I
may stay in school or quit
and I say
it
don' matter much
you wanna mug shot
and the way I feel about it/well
so what?

you got it!

A Song of Sojourner Truth
Dedicated to Bernice Reagon

The trolley cars was rollin and the passengers all white
when Sojourner just decided it was time to take a seat
The trolley cars was rollin and the passengers all white
When Sojourner decided it was time to take a seat
It was time she felt to rest a while and ease up
on her feet
So Sojourner put her hand out
tried to flag the trolley down
So Sojourner put her hand out
for the trolley crossin town
And the driver did not see her
the conductor would not stop
But Sojourner yelled, "It's me!"
And put her body on the track
"It's me!" she yelled, "And yes,
I walked here but I ain walkin back!"
The trolley car conductor and the driver was afraid
to roll right over her and leave her lying dead
So they opened up the car and Sojourner took a seat
So Sojourner sat to rest a while and eased up on her feet

REFRAIN:
Sojourner had to be just crazy
tellin all that kinda truth

I say she musta been plain crazy
plus they say she was uncouth
talkin loud to any crowd
talkin bad insteada sad
She just had to be plain crazy
talkin all that kinda truth

If she had somewhere to go she said
I'll ride
If she had somewhere to go she said
I'll ride
jim crow or no
she said *I'll go*
just like the lady
that she was in all the knowing darkness
of her pride
she said *I'll ride*
she said *I'll talk*
she said *A Righteous Mouth*
ain nothin you should hide
she said she'd ride
just like the lady
that she was in all the knowing darkness
of her pride
she said *I'll ride*

They said she's Black and ugly and they said she's
really rough
They said if you treat her like a dog
well that'll be plenty good enough
And Sojourner said
I'll ride
And Sojourner said
I'll go
I'm a woman and this hell has made me tough
(Thank God!)
This hell has made me tough
I'm a strong Black woman
and Thank God!

REFRAIN:
Sojourner had to be just crazy
tellin all that kinda truth

I say she musta been plain crazy
plus they say she was uncouth
talking loud to any crowd
talkin bad insteada sad
She just had to be plain crazy
talkin all that kinda truth

Alla Tha's All Right, but

Somebody come and carry me into a seven-day kiss
I can' use no historic no national no family bliss
I need an absolutely one to one a seven-day kiss

I can read the daily papers
I can even make a speech
But the news is stuff that tapers
down to salt poured in the breach

I been scheming about my people I been scheming about sex
I been dreaming about Africa and nightmaring Oedipus the Rex
But what I need is quite specific
terrifying rough stuff and terrific

I need an absolutely one to one a seven-day kiss
I can' use no more historic no national no bona fide family bliss
Somebody come and carry me into a seven-day kiss
Somebody come on
Somebody come on and carry me
over there!

Free Flight

Nothing fills me up at night
I fall asleep for one or two hours then
up again my gut
alarms
I must arise
and wandering into the refrigerator
think about evaporated milk homemade vanilla ice cream
cherry pie hot from the oven with Something Like Vermont

Cheddar Cheese disintegrating luscious
on the top while
mildly
I devour almonds and raisins mixed to mathematical
criteria or celery or my very own sweet and sour snack
composed of brie peanut butter honey and
a minuscule slice of party size salami
on a single whole wheat cracker *no salt added*
or I read Cesar Vallejo/Gabriela Mistral/last year's
complete anthology or
I might begin another list of things to do
that starts with toilet paper and
I notice that I never jot down fresh
strawberry shortcake: never
even though fresh strawberry shortcake shoots down
raisins and almonds 6 to nothing
effortlessly
effortlessly
is this poem on my list?
light bulbs lemons envelopes ballpoint refill
post office and zucchini
oranges no
it's not
I guess that means I just forgot
walking my dog around the block leads
to a space in my mind where
during the newspaper strike questions
sizzle through suddenly like
Is there an earthquake down in Ecuador?
Did a TWA supersaver flight to San Francisco
land in Philadelphia instead
or
whatever happened to human rights
in Washington D.C.? Or what about downward destabilization
of the consumer price index
and I was in this school P.S. Tum-Ta-Tum and time came
for me to leave but
No! I couldn't leave: The Rule was anybody leaving
the premises without having taught somebody something
valuable would be henceforth proscribed from the
premises would be forever null and void/dull and
vilified well

I had stood in front of 40 to 50 students running my
mouth and I had been generous with deceitful smiles/soft-
spoken and pseudo-gentile wiles if and when forced
into discourse amongst such adults as constitutes
the regular treacheries of On The Job Behavior
ON THE JOB BEHAVIOR
is this poem on that list
polish shoes file nails coordinate tops and bottoms
lipstick control no
screaming I'm bored because
this is whoring away the hours of god's creation
pay attention to your eyes your hands the twilight
sky in the institutional big windows
no
I did not presume I was not so bold as to put this
poem on that list
then at the end of the class this boy gives me Mahler's 9th
symphony the double album listen
to it let it seep into you he
says transcendental love
he says
I think naw
I been angry all day long/nobody did the assignment
I am not prepared
I am not prepared for so much grace
the catapulting music of surprise that makes me
hideaway my face
nothing fills me up at night
yesterday the houseguest left a brown
towel in the bathroom for tonight
I set out a blue one and
an off-white washcloth seriously
I don't need no houseguest
I don't need no towels/lovers
I just need a dog

Maybe I'm kidding

Maybe I need a woman
a woman be so well you know so wifelike
so more or less motherly so listening so much
the universal skin you love to touch and who the
closer she gets to you the better she looks to me/somebody

say yes and make me laugh and tell me she know she
been there she spit bullets at my enemies she say you
need to sail around Alaska fuck it all try this new
cerebral tea and take a long bath

Maybe I need a man
a man be so well you know so manly so lifelike
so more or less virile so sure so much the deep
voice of opinion and the shoulders like a window
seat and cheeks so closely shaven by a twin-edged
razor blade no oil hair and no dandruff besides/
somebody say yes and make
me laugh and tell me he know he been there he spit
bullets at my enemies he say you need to sail around
Alaska fuck it all and take a long bath

lah-ti-dah and lah-ti-dum
what's this socialized obsession with the bathtub

Maybe I just need to love myself myself
(anyhow I'm more familiar with the subject)
Maybe when my cousin tells me you remind me
of a woman past her prime maybe I need
to hustle my cousin into a hammerlock
position make her cry out uncle and
I'm sorry
Maybe when I feel this horrible
inclination to kiss folks I despise
because the party's like that
an occasion to be kissing people
you despise maybe I should tell them kindly
kiss my

Maybe when I wake up in the middle of the night
I should go downstairs
dump the refrigerator contents on the floor
and stand there in the middle of the spilled milk
and the wasted butter spread beneath my dirty feet
writing poems
writing poems
maybe I just need to love myself myself and
anyway
I'm working on it

Letter to My Friend the Poet Ntozake Shange

Just back from Minnesota/North Dakota
All my clothes into the laundry or
dry cleaners before I leave
again
for Oregon then California
and my agent calls to say your business
manager is sending me
a Christmas present
from you
by messenger
within the next two hours: will
I be home?

Jesus Christ (I think) getting nervous
about two hours housebound
under the circumstances
maybe
one of us
better slow down!

En Passant

A white man tells me he told a white woman

You need to be fucked to death
You need a Black man

She said: What would my family say?

I say the same thing: What would my family
say
about that?

A Short Note to My Very Critical and Well-Beloved Friends and Comrades

First they said I was too light
Then they said I was too dark
Then they said I was too different
Then they said I was too much the same
Then they said I was too young
Then they said I was too old
Then they said I was too interracial
Then they said I was too much a nationalist
Then they said I was too silly
Then they said I was too angry
Then they said I was too idealistic
Then they said I was too confusing altogether:
Make up your mind! They said. Are you militant
or sweet? Are you vegetarian or meat? Are you straight
or are you gay?

And I said, Hey! It's not about *my* mind.

Rape Is Not a Poem

1
One day she saw them coming into the garden
where the flowers live.
They
found the colors beautiful and
they discovered the sweet smell
that the flowers held
so
they stamped upon and tore apart
the garden
just because (they said)
those flowers?
They were asking for it.

2
I let him into the house to say hello.
"Hello," he said.
"Hello," I said.
"How're you?" he asked me.
"Not bad," I told him.
"You look great," he smiled.
"Thanks; I've been busy: I am busy."
"Well, I guess I'll be heading out, again,"
he said.
"Okay," I answered and, "Take care," I said.
"I'm gonna do just that," he said.
"No!" I said: "No! Please don't. Please
leave me alone. Now. No. Please!" I said.
"I'm leaving," he laughed: "I'm leaving you
alone; I'm going now!"
"No!" I cried: "No. Please don't do this to me!"
But he was not talking anymore and there was
nothing else that I could say
to make him listen
to me.

3
And considering your contempt
And considering my hatred consequent to that
And considering the history
that leads us to this dismal place where (your arm
raised
and my eyes
lowered)
there is nothing left but the drippings
of power and
a consummate wreck of tenderness/I
want to know:
Is this what you call
Only Natural?

4
My dog will never learn the names
of stars or thorns but
fully he
encounters whatever it is

shits on the ground
then finds a fallen leaf still holding
raindrops from the day and
there he stays
a big dog
(licking at the tiny water)
delicate as he is
elsewhere
fierce

You should let him teach you how
to come down

Memo:

When I hear some woman say she
has finally decided you can spend time with
other women, I wonder what she means: Her
mother? My mother?
I've always despised my woman friends. Even
if they introduced me to a man I found
attractive I have never let them become
what you could call my intimates. Why
should I? Men are the ones with the money and
the big way with waiters and the passkey
to excitement in strange places of real
danger and the power to make things happen
like babies or war and all these great ideas
about mass magazines for members of the weaker sex
who need permission
to eat potatoes or a doctor's opinion on orgasm after death
or the latest word on what the female
executive should do, after hours, wearing
what. They must be morons: women!
Don't you think?
I guess you could say
I'm stuck in my ways
as
That Cosmopolitan Girl.

What Is This in Reference To?
or
We Must Get Together Sometime Soon!

Hello.
I'm sorry.
I can't talk to you.
I am unavailable.
I am out of the house.
I am out of town.
I am out of the country.
I am out of my mind.
I am indisposed.
The cat has my tongue.
Please do not hang up.
I know this is frustrating
          ridiculous
          solipsistic
          inconvenient
          mechanical
          and
          a pain in the ass
Please listen for the beep.
When you hear the beep
please leave a message as long as you like
or better still
please leave a brief message
or better yet
state your purpose in concise
readily decipherable terms and be sure
to leave your name your number
the time
the date
the place
and a list of the secret desires underlying this conventional
even hackneyed outreach represented
by
your call.
This is your dime.
Listen for the beep. Sucker.

Poem about My Rights

Even tonight and I need to take a walk and clear
my head about this poem about why I can't
go out without changing my clothes my shoes
my body posture my gender identity my age
my status as a woman alone in the evening/
alone on the streets/alone not being the point/
the point being that I can't do what I want
to do with my own body because I am the wrong
sex the wrong age the wrong skin and
suppose it was not here in the city but down on the beach/
or far into the woods and I wanted to go
there by myself thinking about God/or thinking
about children or thinking about the world/all of it
disclosed by the stars and the silence:
I could not go and I could not think and I could not
stay there
alone
as I need to be
alone because I can't do what I want to do with my own
body and
who in the hell set things up
like this
and in France they say if the guy penetrates
but does not ejaculate then he did not rape me
and if after stabbing him if after screams if
after begging the bastard and if even after smashing
a hammer to his head if even after that if he
and his buddies fuck me after that
then I consented and there was
no rape because finally you understand finally
they fucked me over because I was wrong I was
wrong again to be me being me where I was/wrong
to be who I am
which is exactly like South Africa
penetrating into Namibia penetrating into
Angola and does that mean I mean how do you know if
Pretoria ejaculates what will the evidence look like the
proof of the monster jackboot ejaculation on Blackland
and if
after Namibia and if after Angola and if after Zimbabwe

and if after all of my kinsmen and women resist even to
self-immolation of the villages and if after that
we lose nevertheless what will the big boys say will they
claim my consent:
Do You Follow Me: We are the wrong people of
the wrong skin on the wrong continent and what
in the hell is everybody being reasonable about
and according to the *Times* this week
back in 1966 the C.I.A. decided that they had this problem
and the problem was a man named Nkrumah so they
killed him and before that it was Patrice Lumumba
and before that it was my father on the campus
of my Ivy League school and my father afraid
to walk into the cafeteria because he said he
was wrong the wrong age the wrong skin the wrong
gender identity and he was paying my tuition and
before that
it was my father saying I was wrong saying that
I should have been a boy because he wanted one/a
boy and that I should have been lighter skinned and
that I should have had straighter hair and that
I should not be so boy crazy but instead I should
just be one/a boy and before that
it was my mother pleading plastic surgery for
my nose and braces for my teeth and telling me
to let the books loose to let them loose in other
words
I am very familiar with the problems of the C.I.A.
and the problems of South Africa and the problems
of Exxon Corporation and the problems of white
America in general and the problems of the teachers
and the preachers and the F.B.I. and the social
workers and my particular Mom and Dad/I am very
familiar with the problems because the problems
turn out to be
me
I am the history of rape
I am the history of the rejection of who I am
I am the history of the terrorized incarceration of
my self
I am the history of battery assault and limitless
armies against whatever I want to do with my mind

and my body and my soul and
whether it's about walking out at night
or whether it's about the love that I feel or
whether it's about the sanctity of my vagina or
the sanctity of my national boundaries
or the sanctity of my leaders or the sanctity
of each and every desire
that I know from my personal and idiosyncratic
and indisputably single and singular heart
I have been raped
be-
cause I have been wrong the wrong sex the wrong age
the wrong skin the wrong nose the wrong hair the
wrong need the wrong dream the wrong geographic
the wrong sartorial I
I have been the meaning of rape
I have been the problem everyone seeks to
eliminate by forced
penetration with or without the evidence of slime and/
but let this be unmistakable this poem
is not consent I do not consent
to my mother to my father to the teachers to
the F.B.I. to South Africa to Bedford-Stuy
to Park Avenue to American Airlines to the hardon
idlers on the corners to the sneaky creeps in
cars
I am not wrong: Wrong is not my name
My name is my own my own my own
and I can't tell you who the hell set things up like this
but I can tell you that from now on my resistance
my simple and daily and nightly self-determination
may very well cost you your life

Grand Army Plaza
For Ethelbert

Why would anybody build a monument to civil war?

The tall man and myself tonight
we will not sleep together

we may not
either one of us
sleep
in any case
the differential between friend and lover
is a problem
definitions curse
as *nowadays we're friends*
or
we were lovers once
while
overarching the fastidious the starlit
dust
that softens space between us
is the history that bleeds
through shirt and blouse
alike

the stain of skin on stone

But on this hard ground curved by memories
of union and disunion and of brothers dead
by the familiar hand
how do we face to face a man
a woman
interpenetrated
free
and reaching still toward the kiss that will
not suffocate?

We are not survivors of a civil war

We survive our love
because we go on

loving

PART THREE

FROM
Living Room

From Sea to Shining Sea

1
Natural order is being restored
Natural order means you take a pomegranate
that encapsulated plastic looking orb complete
with its little top/a childproof cap that you can
neither twist nor turn
and you keep the pomegranate stacked inside a wobbly
pyramid composed by 103 additional pomegranates
next to a sign saying 89 cents
each

Natural order is being restored
Natural order does not mean a pomegranate
split open to the seeds sucked by the tongue and lips
while teeth release the succulent sounds
of its voluptuous disintegration

The natural order is not about a good time
This is not a good time to be against
the natural order

* * * *

*"Those Black bitches tore it up! Yakkety
yakkety complain complaints couldn't see
no further than they got to have this
they got to have that they got to have
my job, Jack: my job!"*

*"To me it was Black men laid us wide open for the cut.
Busy telling us to go home. Sit tight.
Be sweet. So busy hanging tail and chasing
tail they didn't have no time to take a good
look at the real deal."*

*"Those macho bastards! They would rather blow
the whole thing up than give a little: It was
vote for spite: vote white for spite!"*

*"Fucken feminists turned themselves into bulldagger
dykes and scared the shit out of decent
smalltown people: That's what happened."*

*"Now I don't even like niggers but there they were
chewing into the middle of my paycheck
and not me but a lot of other white people
just got sick of it, sick of carrying
the niggers."*

*"Old men run the government: You think that's
their problem?
Everyone of them is old and my parents and the old
people get out big numbers of them, voting for the dead"*

*"He's eighteen just like all the rest.
Only thing he wants is a girl and a stereo
and hanging out hanging out. What
does he care about the country? What
did he care?"*

Pomegranates 89¢ each

2
Frozen cans of orange juice.
Pre-washed spinach.
Onions by the bag.
Fresh pineapple with a printed
message from the import company.
Cherry tomatoes by the box.
Scallions rubberbanded by the bunch.
Frozen cans of orange juice.
Napkins available.
No credit please.

3
This is not such a hot
time for you or for me.

4
Natural order is being restored.
Designer jeans will be replaced by the designer
of the jeans.
Music will be replaced by reproduction
of the music.
Food will be replaced by information.
Above all the flag is being replaced by the flag.

5
This was not a good time to be gay

Shortly before midnight a Wednesday
massacre felled eight homosexual Americans
and killed two: One man was on his way
to a delicatessen and the other
on his way to a drink. Using an Israeli
submachine gun the killer fired into the crowd
later telling police about the serpent in the garden
of his bloody heart, and so forth

This was not a good time to be Black

Yesterday the Senate passed an anti-busing
rider and this morning the next head
of the Senate Judiciary said he would work
to repeal the Voter Registration
Act and this afternoon the Greensboro
jury fully acquitted members of the Klan
and the American Nazi party in the murder
of 5 citizens and in Youngstown Ohio and in
Chattanooga
Tennessee and in Brooklyn and in Miami
and in Salt Lake City and in Portland Oregon
and in Detroit Michigan
and in Los Angeles and in Buffalo
Black American women and men
were murdered and the hearts
of two of the victims were carved
from the bodies of the victims, etcetera

This was not a good time to be old

Streamliner plans for the Federal Budget
include elimination of Social Security
as it exists; and similarly Medicare and Medicaid
face severe reevaluation, among other things.

This was not a good time to be young

Streamliner plans also include elimination
of the Office of Education and the military
draft becomes a drastic concern as the national
leadership boasts that this country will no longer
be bullied and blackmailed by wars for liberation
or wars
for independence elsewhere on the planet, and the like.

This was not a good time to be a pomegranate ripening on a tree

This was not a good time to be a child

Suicide rates among the young reached
alltime highs as the incidence of child
abuse and sexual abuse
rose dramatically across the nation.
In Atlanta Georgia at least twenty-eight Black
children have been murdered, with
several more missing and all of them feared dead, or
something of the sort.

This was not a good time to be without a job

Unemployment Compensation and the minimum
wage have been identified as programs
that plague the poor and the young
who really require different incentives
towards initiative/pluck and so forth

This was not a good time to have a job

Promising to preserve traditional
values of freedom, the new administration
intends to remove safety regulations
that interfere
with productivity potential, etcetera.

This was not a good time to be a woman

Pursuing the theme of traditional values of freedom
the new leadership has pledged its
opposition to the Equal Rights Amendment
that would in the words of the President-elect
only throw the weaker sex into a vulnerable
position among mischievous men, and the like.

This was not a good time to live in Queens

Trucks carrying explosive nuclear wastes will
exit from the Long Island Expressway and then
travel through residential streets of Queens
en route to the 59th Street Bridge, and so on.

This was not a good time to live in Arkansas

Occasional explosions caused by mystery
nuclear missiles have been cited
as cause for local alarm, among
other things.

This was not a good time to live in Grand Forks North Dakota

Given the presence of a United States nuclear
missile base in Grand Forks North Dakota
the non-military residents of the area feel
that they are living only a day by day distance
from certain
annihilation, etcetera.

This was not a good time to be married.

The Pope has issued directives concerning
lust that make for difficult interaction
between otherwise interested parties

This was not a good time not to be married.
This was not a good time to buy a house
at 18% interest.
This was not a good time to rent housing
on a completely decontrolled
rental market.
This was not a good time to be a Jew
when the national Klan agenda targets
Jews as well as Blacks among its
enemies of the purity of the people
This was not a good time to be a tree
This was not a good time to be a river
This was not a good time to be found with a gun
This was not a good time to be found without one
This was not a good time to be gay
This was not a good time to be Black

This was not a good time to be a pomegranate
or an orange
This was not a good time to be against
the natural order

       —Wait a minute—

6
Sucked by the tongue and the lips
while the teeth release the succulence
of all voluptuous disintegration
I am turning under the trees
I am trailing blood into the rivers
I am walking loud along the streets
I am digging my nails and my heels into the land
I am opening my mouth
I am just about to touch the pomegranates
piled up precarious

7
This is a good time
This is the best time
This is the only time to come together

                                            Fractious
                                            Kicking
                                            Spilling
                                            Burly
                                            Whirling
                                            Raucous
                                            Messy

                                            Free

Exploding like the seeds of a natural disorder.

Des Moines Iowa Rap

So his wife and his daughters could qualify
Lester Williams told the people he was gonna try suicide:
suicide
He promised the papers he would definitely try
so his wife and his babies could qualify for welfare

in the new year.
Welfare.
In the new year.

I wanna job so bad I can taste it I won't waste it
Wanna job so bad

36 years old and home from the Navy
Take my blood, he said, and my bones, he said,
for the meat and the gravy/I'm a vet from the Navy!
Take my meat. Take my bones.
I'm a blood, he said.

Tried suicide. Tried suicide.

Lester Williams made the offer and the offer made news
Wasn't all that much to dispute and confuse
Wouldn't hide in no closet and under no bed
Said he'd straightaway shoot himself dead instead
Like a man
Like a natural man
Like a natural man wanna job so bad he
can taste it
he can taste it

Took the wife in his arms. Held the children in his heart.
Took the gun from his belt. Held the gun to his head.
Like a man.
Like a natural man.
Like a natural man wanna job so bad gotta waste it.
Gotta waste it.

Tried Suicide.
Tried Suicide.

First Poem from Nicaragua Libre: teotecacinte

Can you say Teotecacinte?
Can you say it,
Teotecacinte?

Into the dirt she fell
she blew up the shell
fell into the dirt the artillery
shell blew up the girl
crouching near to the well of the little house
with the cool roof thatched on the slant
the little girl of the little house fell
beside the well unfinished for water
when that mortar
shattered the dirt under her barefeet
and scattered pieces of her four
year old anatomy
into the yard dust and up
among the lower branches of a short tree

Can you say it?

That is two and a half inches of her scalp there
with the soft hairs stiffening
in the grass

Teotecacinte
Can you say it,
Teotecacinte?

Can you say it?

from Nicaragua Libre: photograph of managua

The man is not cute.
The man is not ugly.
The man is teaching himself
to read.
He sits in a kitchen chair
under a banana tree.
He holds the newspaper.
He tracks each word with a finger
and opens his mouth to the sound.
Next to the chair the old V-Z rifle
leans at the ready.

His wife chases a baby pig with a homemade
broom and then she chases her daughter running
behind the baby pig.
His neighbor washes up with water from the barrel
after work.
The dirt floor of his house has been swept.
The dirt around the chair where he sits
has been swept.
He has swept the dirt twice.
The dirt is clean.
The dirt is his dirt.
The man is not cute.
The man is not ugly.
The man is teaching himself
to read.

Problems of Translation:
Problems of Language
Dedicated to Myriam Díaz-Diocaretz

1
I turn to my Rand McNally Atlas.
Europe appears right after the Map of the World.
All of Italy can be seen page 9.
Half of Chile page 29.
I take out my ruler.
In global perspective Italy
amounts to less than half an inch.
Chile measures more than an inch and a quarter
of an inch.
Aproximately
Chile is as long as China
is wide:
Back to the Atlas:
Chunk of China page 17.
All of France page 5: As we say in New York:
Who do France and Italy know
at Rand McNally?

2
I see the four mountains in Chile higher
than any mountain of North America.
I see Ojos del Salado the highest.
I see Chile unequivocal as crystal thread.
I see the Atacama Desert dry in Chile more than the rest
of the world is dry.
I see Chile dissolving into water.
I do not see what keeps the blue land of Chile
out of blue water.
I do not see the hand of Pablo Neruda on the blue land.

3
As the plane flies flat to the trees
below Brazil
below Bolivia
below five thousand miles below
my Brooklyn windows
and beside the shifted Pacific waters
welled away from the Atlantic at Cape Horn
La Isla Negra that is not an island La
Isla Negra
that is not black
is stone and stone of Chile
feeding clouds to color
scale and undertake terrestial forms
of everything unspeakable.

4
In your country how
do you say copper
for my country?

5
Blood rising under the Andes and above
the Andes blood
spilling down the rock
corrupted by the amorality
of so much space
that leaves such little trace of blood
rising to the irritated skin the face
of the confession far
from home:

I confess I did not resist interrogation.
I confess that by the next day I was no longer sure
of my identity
I confess I knew the hunger.
I confess I saw the guns.
I confess I was afraid.
I confess I did not die.

6
What you Americans call a boycott
of the junta?
Who will that feed?

7
Not just the message but the sound.

8
Early morning now and I remember
corriente a la madrugada from a different
English poem,
I remember from the difficulties of the talk
an argument
athwart the wine the dinner and the dancing
meant to welcome you
you did not understand the commonplace expression
of my heart:

the truth is in the life
la verdad de la vida

Early morning:
Do you say *la mañanita?*
But then we lose
the idea of the sky uncurling to the light:

Early morning and I do not think we lose:
the rose we left behind
broken to a glass of water on the table
at the restaurant stands
even sweeter
por la mañanita

Poem on the Road; for Alice Walker

1 On the Road
Once in awhile
it's like calling home long distance but nobody
lives there anymore

2 New Hampshire
White mountains or trout
streams or rocks sharp as a fighter plane
simply afloat
above the superhighways

Almost by herself
(trying to "live free or die")
a white girl twitching white tears
unpolluted under the roar
of Pease Air Force Base immortalized
by flyboys taking out Hiroshima
but now
real interested just to take her out
anywhere at all

This is not racist

3 Brooklyn
Running imagery through the arteries of her
pictures posted up against apartheid
what does a young Black poet do?
What does a young
Black woman poet
do
after dark?

Six dollars in her backpack
carrying the streets like a solitary
sentinel possessed by visions
of new arms new
partners

what does she do?

What does the Black man
in his early thirties
in a bomber jacket
what does the Black man do about the poet
when he sees her?
After he took the six
dollars
After he punched her
down
After he pushed for pussy
After he punctured her lungs with his knife
After the Black man
in his early thirties
in a bomber jacket
After she stopped bleeding
After she stopped pleading
(*please don't hurt me*)

what was the imagery running
through the arteries of the heart
of that partner?

This is not racist

4 New Bedford
The lady wanted to have a drink
The lady wanted to have two drinks

Four men dragged the lady to the table
Two men blocked the door
All of them laughing
Four men
Two men
All of them laughing
A lot of the time the lady could not
breathe
A lot of the time the lady wanted
to lose consciousness

Six men
One lady

All of them Portuguese

This is a promise I am making
it here
legs spread on the pool
table of New Bedford

I am not racist

I am raising my knife
to carve out the heart
of no shame

5   On the Road
This is the promise
I am making it here on the road
of my country

I am raising my knife
to carve out the heart
of no shame

The very next move is not mine

A Song for Soweto

At the throat of Soweto
a devil language falls
slashing
claw syllables to shred and leave
raw
the tongue of the young
girl
learning to sing
her own name

Where she would say
                    water
They would teach her to cry
                    blood

Where she would save
> *grass*

They would teach her to crave
> *crawling into the*
> *grave*

Where she would praise
> *father*

They would teach her to pray
> *somebody please*
> *do not take him*
> *away*

Where she would kiss with her mouth
> *my homeland*

They would teach her to swallow
> *this dust*

But words live in the spirit of her face and that sound will no longer yield to imperial erase

Where they would draw
> *blood*

She will drink
> *water*

Where they would deepen
> *the grave*

She will conjure up
> *grass*

Where they would take
> *father and family away*

She will stand
> *under the sun/she will stay*

Where they would teach her to swallow
> *this dust*

She will kiss with her mouth
> *my homeland*

and stay
with the song of Soweto

stay
with the song of Soweto

Song of the Law Abiding Citizen

so hot so hot so hot so what
so hot so what so hot so hot

They made a mistake
I got more than I usually take
I got food stamps food stamps I got
so many stamps in the mail
I thought maybe I should put them on sale
How lucky I am
I got food stamps: Hot damn!
I made up my mind
to be decent and kind
to let my upright character shine
I sent 10,000 food stamps
back to the President (and his beautiful wife)
and I can't pay the rent
but I sent 10,000 food stamps
back to the President (and his beautiful wife)
how lucky I am
hot damn
They made a mistake
for Chrissake
And I gave it away to the President
I thought that was legal I thought that was kind
and I can't pay the rent
but I sent 10,000 food stamps
back back back to the President

so hot so hot so hot so what
so hot so what so hot so hot

Trucks cruisin' down the avenue
carrying nuclear garbage right next to you
and it's legal
it's radioaction ridin' like a regal
load of jewels
past the bars the cruel
school house and the church and if
the trucks wipeout or crash
or even lurch too hard around a corner
we will just be goners

and it's legal
it's radioaction ridin' regal
through the skittery city street
and don't be jittery
because it's legal
radioaction ridin' the road

Avenue A Avenue B Avenue C Avenue D
Avenue of the Americas

so hot so hot so hot so what
so hot so what so hot so hot
so hot so hot so hot so what

October 23, 1983

The way she played the piano
    the one listening was the one taken
    the one taken was the one
        into the water/
        watching the foam
        find the beautiful boulders
        dark
        easily liquid
        and true as the stone
        of that meeting/molecular
        elements of lust
        distilled by the developing
        sound
        sorrow
        sound
        fused by the need of the fingers
        to note down
        to touch upon
        to span
        to isolate
        to pound
        to syncopate
        to sound
        sorrow

        sound
        among the waters
        gathering
        corpuscular/exquisite

constellations tuning among waves
the soul itself
pitched atonal but below
the constellations tuning among waves
the soul itself

a muscular/exquisite

matter of tactful
        exact
          uproarious

heart
collecting the easily dark
liquid
look
of the beautiful boulders

in that gathering
   that water

for a.b.t.

Menu

We got crispy chicken
we got frisky chicken
we got digital chicken
we got Chicken Evergreen

We got chicken salad
we got chicken with rice
we got radar chicken
we got chicken in the first degree

but we ain't got no fried chicken.

We got Chicken Red Light
we got drive-in chicken
we got felony chicken
we got chicken gravy

but we ain't got no fried chicken.

We got half a chicken
we got 2 chickens
we got Chicken Tylenol
we got chicken on ice

but we ain't got no fried chicken.

We got King Chicken
we got chicken a la mode
we got no-lead chicken

We got chainsaw chicken
we got chicken in a chair
we got borderline chicken
we got Chicken for the Young at Heart

We got aeresol chicken
we got Chicken Guitar

but we ain't got no fried chicken.

We got Coast Guard Chicken
we got sixpack chicken
we got Chicken Las Vegas
we got chicken to burn

but we ain't got no fried chicken.

We got 10-speed chicken
we got atomic chicken
we got chicken on tape

We got day-care chicken
we got Chicken Mascara
we got second-hand chicken

but we ain't got no fried chicken.

We got dead chicken
we got chicken on the hoof

we got open admissions chicken
we got Chicken Motel

We got astronaut chicken
we got chicken to go

We got gospel chicken
we got four-wheel drive chicken
we got chain gang chicken
we got chicken transfusions

but we ain't got no fried chicken

We got wrong turn chicken
we got rough draft chicken
we got chicken sodas
we got Chicken Deluxe

but we ain't
got
no

fried chicken.

Copyright © 1983:
    June Jordan & Sara Miles

Addenda to the Papal Bull
Dedicated to the Poet Nicanor Parra

The Pope thinks.
The Pope thinks all of the time.
The Pope thinks it is the duty of His
Holiness to think out loud.
The Pope thinks out loud.
The Pope thinks it is the duty of His
Holiness to publish His thoughts.
The Pope publishes His thoughts.
The Pope is thinking about peace.
He is in favor of peace.
The Pope is thinking about meat.
He is in favor of fish.

The Pope is thinking about women.
He thinks women can be acceptable.
These are the thoughts of the Pope on sex:
The Pope thinks that no sex is better than good.
The Pope thinks that good sex is better than sin.
The Pope thinks that sin happens
when sex happens when two people
want to have sex with each other.
The Pope thinks that is an example of lust.
The Pope thinks that lust is for the birds.
Marriage without sex without lust is permissible.
Remarriage is permissible only
without lackluster and lusty sex, both.
The Pope thinks that these thoughts
on peace and women and meat and sex
deserve our most obedient attention.
The Pope is thinking and thinking and thinking.
Who can deny the usefulness of His concern?

Poem for Guatemala
Dedicated to Rigoberto Manchú

(*With thanks to* Journey to the Depths, *the testimony of Rigoberto Manchú, translated into English by Patricia Goedicke, October, 1982*)

No matter how loudly I call you the sound of your name
makes the day soft
Nothing about it sticks to my throat
Guatemala
syllables that lilt into twilight and lust
Guatemala
syllables to melt bullets

They call you Indian
They called me West Indian
You learned to speak Spanish when I did
We were thirteen
I wore shoes

I ate rice and peas
The beans and the rice in your pot
brought the soldiers
to hack off our arms

"Walk like that into the kitchen!
Walk like that into the clearing!
Girl with no arms!"

I had been playing the piano

Because of the beans and the rice in your pot
the soldiers arrived with an axe
to claim you guerilla
girl with no arms

An Indian is not supposed to own a pot of food
An Indian is too crude
An Indian covers herself with dirt so the cold
times will not hurt her

Cover yourself with no arms!

They buried my mother in New Jersey.
Black cars carried her there.
She wore flowers and a long dress.

Soldiers pushed into your mother
and tore out her tongue
and whipped her under a tree
and planted a fly in the bleeding
places so that worms
spread through the flesh
then the dogs
then the buzzards
then the soldiers laughing
at the family of the girl
with no arms
guerilla girl
with no arms

You go with no arms
among the jungle treacheries
You go with no arms
into the mountains hunting
revenge

I watch you
walk like that
into the kitchen
walk like that
into the clearing
girl with no arms

I am learning new syllables
of revolution

Guatemala
Guatemala
Girl with no arms

On the Real World: Meditation #1.

5 shirts
2 blouses
3 pairs of jeans and the iron's on hot
for cotton:
I press the steam trigger to begin
with the section underneath the collar
from the inside out.
Then the sleeves. Starting with the cuffs.
Now the collar wrong way before it's right.
I'm not doing so good.
Around where the sleeve joins the shoulder looks
funny.
My hand stops startled.
New like a baby there's a howling on the rise.
I switch the shirt so that the iron reaches
the front panel easily.
That howling like a long walk by the Red
Brigades for twenty years between improbable
Chinese ravines with watercolor trees
poked into a spot as graceful as clouds
missing deliberate from a revolutionary land-
scape printed in Japan
ebbs then returns a louder howling cold

as the long walk towards the watery
limits of the whole earth blasted by the air
become tumescent in a lonely place
inhabited by the deaf or the invisible
but querulously looming victims of such speed
in spoken pain the louder howling large
as the original canvas containing that landscape
printed in Japan almost overloaded as the howling loses
even its small voice while I
bite my lips and lower my head
hard into the ferocity of that sound
dwarfing me into someone almost immaterial
as now I smell fire
and look down all the way to the shirt
pocket
skyblue and slightly burned

Poem on

the snow
nearly as soft
as the sleeping nipple
of your left breast

A Runaway Lil Bit Poem

Sometimes DeLiza get so crazy she omit
the bebop from the concrete she intimidate
the music she excruciate the whiskey she
obliterate the blow she sneeze
hypothetical at sex

Sometimes DeLiza get so crazy she abstruse
about a bar-be-cue ribs wonder-white-bread
sandwich in the car with hot sauce
make the eyes roll right to where you are
fastidious among the fried-up chicken wings

Sometimes DeLiza get so crazy she exasperate
on do they hook it up they being Ingrid
Bergman and some paranoid schizophrenic Mister
Gregory Peck-peck: Do
they hook it up?

Sometimes DeLiza get so crazy she drive
right across the water flying champagne bottles
from the bridge she last drink to close the bars she
holler kissey lips she laugh she let
you walk yourself away:

Sometimes DeLiza get so crazy!

DeLiza Questioning Perplexities:

If Dustin Hoffaman prove
a father be a better mother than a mother

If Dustin Hoffaman prove
a man be a better woman than a woman

When do she get to see
a Betterman than Hoffaman?

Poem Towards a Final Solution

In a press conference this afternoon the Secretary
of Space Development confirmed earlier reports
of a comprehensive plan nearing completion
in his Office.

Scheduled to meet with the President later
this week, Mr. Samuel B. Fierce the Third
jokingly termed the forthcoming package of proposals
"A Doozie".

The following represents a news team summary
of his remarks:

His Office will issue findings of a joint survey
of all National Parks conducted in cooperation with
the Department of the Interior in an effort to delimit
unnecessary vegetation.

His Office will recommend installation of nuclear
reactors inside low-growth residential areas of American
cities in order to encourage voluntary citizen re-
location at estimated savings to the Federal Government
of more than 2 billion dollars, yearly.

At the same time, Mr. Fierce suggested that he will
recommend
quick phasing out of Federal programs for
land reclamation
described by the Secretary at one particularly
light-hearted
moment during the press conference as
"Neanderthal nostalgia
for the little flowers that grow."

In addition, the Secretary indicated he will call
for the computation of food stamps as income so that,
for example, a legitimate Welfare recipient in Mississippi
will have exactly $8. a month as disposable cash.

Finally, Mr. Fierce alluded to a companion proposal
that will raise the rent for subsidized housing by 20%.

These various initiatives can be trusted to contribute
significantly to the President's economic goals and to
the development of more space, coast to coast. They
will furthermore establish the Office of
Space Development
as an increasingly powerful factor in budget-conscious
policymaking.

An unidentified reporter then queried the Secretary as to
whether this plan could fairly be translated as take
down the trees, tear-up the earth, evacuate the urban poor,
and let the people hang, generally speaking.

Mr. Fierce dismissed the question as a clear-cut attempt
at misleading and alarmist language deliberately obtuse
to the main objective of economic recovery for the nation.

Pending official release of his recommendations to
the President, the Secretary refused to comment on
the snow
falling on the stones of the cities everywhere.

Apologies to All the People in Lebanon
*Dedicated to the 600,000 Palestinian men, women, and children
who lived in Lebanon from 1948–1983.*

I didn't know and nobody told me and what
could I do or say, anyway?

They said you shot the London Ambassador
and when that wasn't true
they said so
what
They said you shelled their northern villages
and when U.N. forces reported that was not true
because your side of the cease-fire was holding
since more than a year before
they said so
what
They said they wanted simply to carve
a 25 mile buffer zone and then
they ravaged your
water supplies your electricity your
hospitals your schools your highways and byways all
the way north to Beirut because they said this
was their quest for peace
They blew up your homes and demolished the grocery
stores and blocked the Red Cross and took away doctors
to jail and they cluster-bombed girls and boys
whose bodies
swelled purple and black into twice the original size
and tore the buttocks from a four month old baby
and then
they said this was brilliant

military accomplishment and this was done
they said in the name of self-defense they said
that is the noblest concept
of mankind isn't that obvious?
They said something about never again and then
they made close to one million human beings homeless
in less than three weeks and they killed or maimed
40,000 of your men and your women and your children

But I didn't know and nobody told me and what
could I do or say, anyway?

They said they were victims. They said you were
Arabs.
They called   your apartments and gardens   guerilla
strongholds.
They called   the screaming devastation
that they created   the rubble.
Then they told you to leave, didn't they?

Didn't you read the leaflets that they dropped
from their hotshot fighter jets?
They told you to go.
One hundred and thirty-five thousand
Palestinians in Beirut and why
didn't you take the hint?
Go!
There was the Mediterranean: You
could walk into the water and stay
there.
What was the problem?

I didn't know and nobody told me and what
could I do or say, anyway?

Yes, I did know it was the money I earned as a poet that
paid
for the bombs and the planes and the tanks
that they used to massacre your family

But I am not an evil person
The people of my country aren't so bad

You can't expect but so much
from those of us who have to pay taxes and watch
American tv

You see my point;

I'm sorry.
I really am sorry.

Another Poem About the Man

the man who brought you the garbage can
                the graveyard
                the grossout
                the grimgram
                the grubby grabbing
                bloody blabbing nightly news
                now brings you
                Grenada

helicopters grating nutmeg trees
rifles shiny on the shellshocked sand
the beautiful laundry of the bombs falling into fresh air
artillery and tanks up against a halfnaked girl
and her boyfriend

another great success
brought to you
by trash delivering more trash to smash
and despoil the papaya
the breadfruit and bloodroot
shattered and bloodspattered
from freedom
rammed down the throat
of Grenada now Grenada she
no sing no more
Grenada now Grenada she
no sing no more she lose
she sky
to yankee invaders
Grenada now Grenada she
no sing no more

Poor Form

That whole way to Delphi
The children wrecked loaves of bread
smeared cheese banged each other
on the nose
and I must admit
I tried to obliterate such dread
disturbance of the dead the bother
of the beeline to the rose
the yowling of the healthy

Hoping to hear the gods
Having to wait on goats
we drove
not very fast
against the freeze that height promotes
the odds
against the living
that don't last

In bed
your hair beside my face
I do not sing
instead
I brace against the ending

Test of Atlanta 1979—

What kind of a person would kill Black children?
What kind of a person could persuade eighteen
different Black children to get into a car or
a truck or a van?
What kind of a person could kill or kidnap
these particular
Black children:
              Edward Hope Smith, 14 years old, dead
              Alfred James Evans, 14 years old, dead
              Yosef Bell, 9 years old, dead
              Milton Harvey, 14 years old, dead

> Angel Lanier, 12 years old, dead
> Eric Middlebrooks, 14 years old, dead
> Christopher Richardson, 11 years old, dead
> Aaron Wyche, 11 years old, dead
> LaTanya Wilson, 7 years old, dead
> Anthony B. Carter, 9 years old, dead
> Earl Lee Terrell, 10 years old, dead
> Clifford Jones, 13 years old, dead
> Aaron Jackson, Jr., 9 years old, dead
> Patrick Rogers, 16 years old, dead
> Charles Stevens, 12 years old, dead
> Jeffrey Lamar Mathis, 10 years old, missing
> Darron Glass, 10 years old, missing
> Lubie "Chuck" Geter, 14 years old, dead

What kind of a person could kill a Black child
and then kill another Black child and then
kill another Black child and then kill another
Black child and then kill another
Black child and then kill another Black
child
and stay above suspicion?
What about the police?
What about somebody Black?
What sixteen year old would say no to a cop?
What seven year old would say no thanks to me?
What is an overreaction to murder?
What kind of a person could kill a Black
child and then kill a Black child and then
kill a Black child?

What kind of a person are you?
What kind of a person am I?

What makes you so sure?

What kind of a person could save a Black child?

What kind of a people will lay down its
life for the lives of our children?

What kind of a people are we?

Relativity

It's 5 after 4 a.m. and nothing but my own
motion stirs throughout the waiting air
the rain completely purged earlier and all
day long. I could call
you now but that would join you to this
restless lying down and getting up to list
still another act I must commit
tomorrow if I ever sleep if I ever stop
sleeping long enough to act upon the space
between this comatose commotion
and the next time I can look into your
face. I hope you're laughing at the cans
of soup the house to clean the kitchen curtains
I will wash and iron
like so many other promises I make
myself: to sweep the stairs down
to the front door
and to answer every letter down to no
thanks.
     My own motion
does not satisfy tonight and later
in the daylight I'll be speeding through the streets
a secret messenger a wakeup agent walking
backwards maybe walking sideways
but for damn sure headed possibly southeast
as well as every other whichway
in your absolute
direction

Home: January 29, 1984

I can tell
because the ashtray was cleaned out
because the downstairs coconut is still full of milk
because actually nothing was left
except two shells hinged together pretty tough

at the joint
I can tell
because the in-house music now includes
the lying down look of gold and your shoulders
because there is no more noise in my head
because one room two hallways two flights of stairs
and the rest of northamerica remain
to be seen in this movie about why
I am trying to write this poem

                                          not a letter
                                          not a proclamation
                                          not a history

I am trying to write this poem
because I can tell
because it's way after midnight and so what
I can tell
eyes open or shut
I can tell
George Washington did not sleep
here
I can tell
it was you
I can tell
it really was
you

Nightline: September 20, 1982

"I know it's an unfortunate way to say it, but
do you think you can put this massacre
on the back burner now?"

Moving Towards Home
"Where is Abu Fadi," she wailed.
"Who will bring me my loved one?"
   New York Times 9/20/82

I do not wish to speak about the bulldozer and the
red dirt
not quite covering all of the arms and legs
Nor do I wish to speak about the nightlong screams
that reached
the observation posts where soldiers lounged about
Nor do I wish to speak about the woman who shoved
her baby
into the stranger's hands before she was led away
Nor do I wish to speak about the father whose sons
were shot
through the head while they slit his own throat before
the eyes
of his wife
Nor do I wish to speak about the army that lit continuous
flares into the darkness so that the others could see
the backs of their victims lined against the wall
Nor do I wish to speak about the piled up bodies and
the stench
that will not float
Nor do I wish to speak about the nurse again and
again raped
before they murdered her on the hospital floor
Nor do I wish to speak about the rattling bullets that
did not
halt on that keening trajectory
Nor do I wish to speak about the pounding on the
doors and
the breaking of windows and the hauling of families into
the world of the dead
I do not wish to speak about the bulldozer and the
red dirt
not quite covering all of the arms and legs
because I do not wish to speak about unspeakable events
that must follow from those who dare
"to purify" a people
those who dare

"to exterminate" a people
those who dare
to describe human beings as "beasts with two legs"
those who dare
"to mop up"
"to tighten the noose"
"to step up the military pressure"
"to ring around" civilian streets with tanks
those who dare
to close the universities
to abolish the press
to kill the elected representatives
of the people who refuse to be purified
those are the ones from whom we must redeem
the words of our beginning
because I need to speak about home
I need to speak about living room
where the land is not bullied and beaten into
a tombstone
I need to speak about living room
where the talk will take place in my language
I need to speak about living room
where my children will grow without horror
I need to speak about living room where the men
of my family between the ages of six and sixty-five
are not
marched into a roundup that leads to the grave
I need to talk about living room
where I can sit without grief without wailing aloud
for my loved ones
where I must not ask where is Abu Fadi
because he will be there beside me
I need to talk about living room
because I need to talk about home

I was born a Black woman
and now
I am become a Palestinian
against the relentless laughter of evil
there is less and less living room
and where are my loved ones?

It is time to make our way home.

ALSO PUBLISHED BY VIRAGO

MOVING TOWARDS HOME

Political Essays

June Jordan

'A major and indispensable reading experience . . . We see at work the committed, passionate, revolutionary creative mind that will, when embodied in the collective consciousness of us all, help deliver us from the deceptions if not the violence of American life' – *Alice Walker*.

June Jordan – poet, activist, essayist, teacher – is one of the most powerful political writers of our time. In this extraordinary collection of her writings, she gives us a manifesto of hope, anger and visionary power. While ducking police bullets in the Harlem riots of 1964, Jordan realised that she hated everything and everyone white. But at the same time, she recognised that hate was what motivated her enemies. 'So back in 1964,' she writes, 'I resolved not to run on hatred, but, instead, to use what I loved, words, to fight for the people I loved.' The scope of her writing over the past twenty-five years bears vivid witness to her intention: police brutality; the poverty of educational opportunity offered to Black children in the ghettos; witnessing in Mississippi a white man's casual murder of another human being; her mother's death; the viability of Black English; Nicaragua and South Africa; child abuse; the silences of friendship – all summon up Jordan's clear voice and unwavering commitment.

YOU CAN'T DROWN THE FIRE

Latin American Women Writing in Exile

Edited by Alicia Partnoy

'The voice of exile ricochets off endless walls, never losing its resonance or shattering the walls . . . I cannot think of anyone who could have done a better job of gathering up these voices: for Alicia Partnoy is, herself, very much a part of this history. Listen to these women . . . Learn, through their words, what it means to leave your homeland and take it with you at one and the same time' – *Margaret Randall*.

This important and moving anthology brings together contributions from thirty-five Latin American women writing in exile. In essays, stories, poetry, letters and song, they bring us face to face with the horrifying experience of exile, torture and death. Yet these writings are never defeatist. Denouncing political repression, they testify resoundingly to the energy, courage and strength of Latin American women in exile in every corner of the world. *You Can't Drown the Fire* brings home to us the individual differences, as well as the unifying political experiences of struggle voiced by women from Paraguay, Uruguay, Chile, Colombia, Guatemala, Bolivia, Argentina and El Salvador.

INVENTED LIVES

Narratives of Black Women 1860-1960

Mary Helen Washington

'Ms Washington has created a most engaging dialogue between the great Black women writers and herself. This collection is, in fact, two fine books in one: at once an anthology and a critical study' – *New York Times*.

In this marvellous companion volume to her anthology of stories by Black women writers, *Any Woman's Blues,* Mary Helen Washington explores the works, and the worlds, of Black American women writers between 1860 and 1960. Bringing together selected short stories and novel extracts from ten writers – Harriet Jacobs, Frances Ellen Watkins Harper, Pauline E. Hopkins, Fannie Barrier Williams, Marita Bonner, Nella Larsen, Zora Neale Hurston, Ann Petry, Dorothy West and Gwendolyn Brooks – she introduces a remarkable range of voices and draws out the hidden and overt challenges of a body of work rich in cultural, political and literary meaning. *Invented Lives* also includes an Introduction and six chapters in which Mary Helen Washington examines Black women writers' search for a narrative structure appropriate to their experiences in American society. The result is a stunning collection of prose and an eloquent affirmation of a neglected literary tradition.